STUDIES IN INTERNATIONAL SECURITY

*

STUDIES IN INTERNATIONAL SECURITY: 13

AFRICAN ARMIES
AND
CIVIL ORDER

J. M. LEE

Published for The Institute
for Strategic Studies

FREDERICK A. PRAEGER, *Publishers*

New York · Washington

BOOKS THAT MATTER

Published in the United States of America in 1969
by Frederick A. Praeger, Inc., Publishers
111 Fourth Avenue, New York, N.Y. 10003

Library of Congress Catalog Card Number: 69-19720

Printed in Great Britain

CONTENTS

TABLES

A map of Tropical Africa follows the index.

J. M. Lee, at present senior lecturer at the Institute of Commonwealth Studies, University of London, was formerly in the Department of Government at the University of Manchester from 1958 until he finished writing this book in March 1968. He was seconded to Makerere College, Uganda, as a lecturer in 1962–63 and to H M Treasury as a temporary principal in 1968–69. He went to the University of Ghana as a visiting lecturer in the summer of 1963, and apart from the two tours undertaken in the collecting of material for this book, has made three other tours of study in African countries. He is the author of a study of local government in Cheshire, *Social Leaders and Public Persons* (1963), and of British colonial policy, *Colonial Development and Good Government* (1967); both of which were published by the Clarendon Press.

PREFACE

This book was made possible by the generosity of my colleagues in the Department of Government at the University of Manchester, Professors Dennis Austin, Brian Chapman, and S. E. Finer. They agreed to relieve me of most of my teaching duties for two terms during the session 1967–68, in order to give me time to collect material. The book was commissioned by the Institute for Strategic Studies. I am particularly grateful to Alastair Buchan, the Director, and to Brigadier Kenneth Hunt, his Deputy, for their support, interest, and counsel during my work in London and on two short trips to Africa.

The subject imposes many handicaps on an author. To be British, when talking to African soldiers or to the representatives of other powers rendering military assistance, gives one a certain 'colonial identity'. I lack the necessary Marxist reputation to give me an entry into the world of 'liberation movements', nor have I the kind of security clearance given to American scholars when they make a study which has policy implications. Some informants may have led me astray. It is difficult to cross-check matters which are 'sensitive'. I hope I was able to gauge the correct level of credibility, and to make allowances for the difficulties of 'translation', particularly between British and French concepts. The basis of the whole work was that all comment would be unattributable.

My colleagues in the faculty who helped me with statistical analysis, especially Martin Godfrey, will perhaps be disappointed to see such little evidence of their advice in the final text. But it seemed difficult to give the book a statistical basis, when so much of the evidence was fragmentary. I would like to thank Mrs Watts and her colleagues in the Computers Section for undertaking the experimental calculations. I alone am responsible for the treatment which the subject was finally given.

London   J.M.L.
1969

Chapter 1

STATE AND SOCIETY

THE aim of this book is to explain why the new states of tropical Africa are vulnerable to subversion by the armies created to protect them. It assumes that action by members of the security forces in the political life of these countries is a direct consequence of the fact that when power is transferred peacefully from colonial authorities to independent governments, states are likely to be organizations which cannot easily establish acceptable rules for the conduct of public business. This does not mean that new states created by decolonization must always be subject to military intervention, but that the communities living inside boundaries designated by a colonial power will often have little experience of living together, and therefore few opportunities to develop a civil order which avoids being dependent on violence as a means of changing government.

Other and more developed states may occasionally suffer from comparable difficulties, particularly if the rivalries between different communities stultify the growth of a common political language. The absence of civil order is not an inseparable feature of decolonization. There are countries where the transfer of power has led to civilian procedures for effecting changes in political office; and others which have never been subject to colonial rule and yet remain exposed to military intervention. But the chief interest of studying African politics in recent years has been the regularity with which soldiers and policemen have undertaken to use their weapons in an attempt to resolve some of the stubborn conflicts which follow the transfer of power. It, therefore, seems worthwhile to contribute to a general understanding of military participation in politics by looking at the particular circumstances in which African security forces were established and their weapons supplied.

These new governments clearly share many features with those in the Middle East and Latin America where military intervention is common practice. The individual living under their rule belongs more closely to a system of local and family custom than to a political culture which confers common rights of citizenship. These countries in the Middle East, Latin

America and Africa lack the social organizations which in Europe are associated with the middle classes; they have few professionally educated people outside the army and the government. In a large number of countries the state apparatus seems remote from the mass of the people.

But it is equally clear that the behaviour of African soldiers and policemen since 1960 is not in precisely the same mould as the better documented actions of their counterparts in the Middle East or Latin America. Armies in the Middle East since Ataturk have seen themselves as the natural vehicles of social revolution; those in Latin America which claim a certain identity with the state may intervene to prevent the election of a reforming president. Nor is it certain that African security forces must all face the type of insurgent movements which attack governments in Asia. Despite the importance of the guerrilla rebellions in the Camerouns and the Congo, there seems to be no clear pattern in African insurrection. Although Africa presents many opportunities for subversion, it has no exact equivalent of the revolutionary tradition or the intimidation through sects and secret societies associated with the 'unofficial culture' of China and parts of South-east Asia. What are the distinctive features of African behaviour?

Soldiers must be understood in terms of the environment in which they operate. The method followed in this book is the relatively simple one of avoiding too heavy a concentration on individual crises and of stressing the features of state and society which the greater part of tropical Africa appears to share in common. All the states created by the 'peaceful transfer of power' inherited a state apparatus, an army and a police force based on colonial models. The societies contained within the territories, units which were designated as states, have yet to learn a common language of politics which might inhibit military intervention.

These common features make it possible to explain the problems of government and military rule in Africa by reference to a single basic idea – the absence of 'civil order'. This concept is hard to define. Conditions of 'civil order' mean that a sufficient number of people, who acknowledge the authority of the same government, have developed lines of communication within their society to establish a certain respect for the limits of violence as an instrument of politics. Although the use of 'law and order' notions may give a false impression of effective government when the conditions described are approaching anarchy, it is important to employ an approach which emphasizes the nature of the state. 'Civil order' may be a concept which is both legalistic and Eurocentric. Many countries in Europe developed a respect for the limits of political violence, at the same time as the state apparatus was being shaped. Elsewhere, for example, in the United States, the state apparatus came before any recognized conventions on the use of violence.

The 'peaceful transfer of power' in tropical Africa created new states in which the state apparatus itself was the only major expression of political convention. 'Civil Order' is the acceptance of certain norms within a broader definition of the state than that provided by the formal institutions of government, which help to remove the high degree of uncertainty that might otherwise prevail in political negotiations. The attempt to create order in Africa is really a fight to define the limits of political action. Those states which inherited colonial constitutions face in an acute form the dilemmas of this situation. Some of these problems can be isolated and studied.

States created by a revolutionary war have therefore been deliberately excluded from this account. Those created by 'peaceful transfer of power' in fact cover a wide range of situations, from those where 'peaceful' may be taken literally – 'independence' being a convenient device for transferring direct administrative responsibility – to those where the nationalist movements used violence against the colonial authorities. There are no references to the experience of North Africa and the Mahgreb – *l'Afrique Blanche* in French terminology. The Algerian revolution may provide a model for liberation movements south of the Sahara, but the difficulties of the Algerian state are not directly comparable with those of states in tropical Africa. The examples given in this book are taken from thirty countries (see Table Two). These include the eighteen French-speaking African states associated with the European Common Market, as well as Guinea; the ten English-speaking states; and Ethiopia, an historic state whose experience of colonial rule is limited to the period of Italian intervention – the greater part of *l'Afrique Noire*. Although it falls into the Arab sphere of influence, the Sudan has been included because it presents many contrasts with the problems faced by states farther south. No reference will be made to Liberia, or to territories still under colonial rule. The largest military organizations operating in this area are in fact the levies employed in wars against rebels in the Portuguese territories: they number at least 120,000 with two kinds of reservists, a militia and a mobile force.

TABLE ONE

COLONIAL INFANTRY STRUCTURE

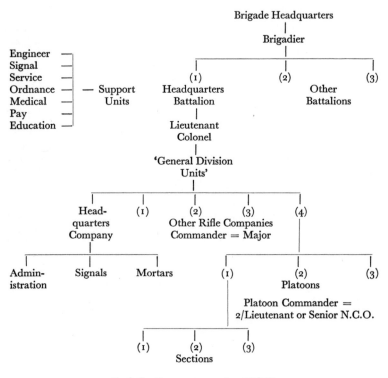

Each Section = 7 men + 1 N.C.O.

KEY

Section	=	8	Normal practice = at least 4 officers
Platoon	=	30	in each company headquarters
Company	=	100	About 55 officers per battalion (35 in
Battalion			GD and 20 support)
with support	=	750+	
Brigade	=	2 or 3 battalions	

TABLE TWO

DEFENCE FORCES: 1967

	Army size	African officers	Expatriate officers	Air Force size	Navy size
Burundi	2,000	60	30	–	–
Cameroun	3,800	120	16	150	110
C.A.R.	1,000	45	15	40	35
Chad	1,500	20	25	50	–
Congo B.	1,900	60	2	75	–
Congo D.R.	35,000	1,500	70	2,000	–
Dahomey	1,750	30	9	18	–
Ethiopia	40,000	3,000	–	2,000	1,200
Gabon	450	18	7	50	25
Gambia	– 600 police		–	–	–
	(150 in mobile units)				
Ghana	14,000	700	4	1,000	1,000
Guinea	5,000	150	–	60	–
Ivory Coast	3,500	120	90	130	110
Kenya	5,000	300	–	450	250
Madagascar	3,750	107	60	70	200
Malawi	1,086	40	20	–	–
Mali	3,000	150	–	20	–
Mauritania	1,400	30	12	21	20
Niger	2,000	30	2	30	–
Nigeria	12,000 *	600	–	1,000	1,500
Ruanda	1,500	60	10	–	–
Senegal	5,000	185	35	170	150
Sierra Leone	1,200	65	10	–	60
Somalia	11,000	325	–	800	180
Sudan	26,500	1,050	–	400	150
Tanzania	5,000	250	–	200	–
Togo	700	17	–	10	–
Uganda	7,000	350	–	350	–
Upper Volta	1,700	58	8	15	–
Zambia	3,900	100	130	240	–
	(29)†			(25)	(14)

* Before civil war: estimates of the wartime army are 50,000 for the federation (some say 80,000) and 14,000 for the Biafran militia.
† Figures in brackets indicate numbers of armies, air forces and navies.

But the armies with which this book is concerned are comparatively small. Apart from Nigeria, which inflated its forces
to fight the war against Biafra, and Ethiopia, which has about
thirty battalions of infantry and a long tradition of military re-
tainers, the largest regular army is that of the Democratic
Republic of the Congo. The latter has twenty-one battalions
of infantry and one battalion of parachutists. Armies which
number more than 5,000 men are rare. The most rapid expansion of security forces has taken place largely in the English-
speaking states. Few can afford to support more than a brigade
of infantry.

The subject has a very short time-span. Evidence for most
countries covers only a decade, or in some cases, barely five years.
There is of course a much longer tradition of military activity in
politics in those states, such as Egypt and the Sudan, which came
under the authority of the Ottoman Empire. The mutiny of the
force publique in the Congo in 1960, and the collapse of the Mali
Federation later in the same year marked the beginning of
political awareness among African soldiers. The first successful
assassination to be undertaken by the discontented was the
murder of the Togolese President, Sylvanus Olympio, in January
1963.

The Congo acquired a symbolic significance for all the new
states of tropical Africa. Aristide Zolberg sees it as the prototype
of what would have happened elsewhere if independence had
been granted without any preparation.[1] It provided a moral
lesson for all new regimes. The state survived because it was
supported by a massive international rescue operation, although
it lacked the means of creating political order. Hugh Tinker
described it as a 'broken-backed state'.

White mercenary troops became the symbol of a state's dependence upon outside powers. The Congolese government was
only able to destroy the movement based on Stanleyville by the
use of mercenary troops. This fact alone humiliated all the new
regimes of tropical Africa which had sent troops to the United
Nations force in the Congo. The rescue operation mounted by the
United States and Belgium to recover those Europeans besieged
in Stanleyville in 1964 provoked great anger among African
leaders. The operation was an insult to their integrity. The
lessons of the Congo were well learnt by its neighbours.

The great powers, and many of the older states in the world

[1] A. R. Zolberg, 'A View of the Congo', *World Politics*, XIX (1), October
1966.

community, are primarily concerned with the effect of internal strife on the international order, not with the 'civil order' of the state itself. Most of the former colonial powers have a natural interest in keeping the successor state apparatus together in the form which it was originally given. Their main fear is becoming involved in a conflict which they have not sought and which may have important consequences for the conduct of diplomatic relations in other fields. Russian and Chinese involvement in the Congo in 1960, and the massive diplomatic effort necessary to mount a United Nations peace-keeping force, brought home to the former colonial powers the fragility of the system of new states which they had been concerned to create. The performance of the armies which the former colonial powers had themselves designed became in some way tied to their own international prestige after 1960. In planning the 'peaceful transfer of power' the colonial authorities assumed that their military presence might be required in the background long after 'independence'. What they did not anticipate was the speed in which this presence would be put to the test.

The major threat to the system of new states is the sponsorship by other powers of rival structures to the successor state apparatus. In the absence of any accepted 'civil order', it is impossible to prevent the opponents of those in power from sponsoring forms of military organizations themselves. The willingness of other outside powers to provide money and supplies for any potential revolutionaries gave substance to this threat. China in 1964 gave extensive support to the Mulelist movement in the Congo; President Nkrumah of Ghana set up training camps for guerrillas who were to be sent to provoke uprisings in neighbouring states. There was no guarantee that the security forces trained by the departing colonial power would be able to retain a monopoly of the instruments of violence.

It is necessary to make two important definitions in order to understand the reality of this basic threat. Both illustrate the nature of the problems involved in the creation of 'civil order'. First, any rival structure constitutes a challenge to the legitimacy of the apparatus for which the departing colonial power was responsible. What rights have the security forces to enforce the decisions of a legitimate government? Second, any rival structure must claim that it is more representative of the whole territorial unit than the officially sponsored body. What basis of support have the security forces among the 'nation' at large? It is precisely the nature of legitimate government and the degree of

B

'national' identity which are in dispute in any situation where 'civil order' is in doubt.

Whenever there is no general agreement about the precise relationship between the state and society, any military organization is obliged to defend its own position and make its own definitions of legitimacy and identity. Each may place its rival in other categories from itself. A 'national liberation movement' regards itself as the legitimate representative of the people; and the so-called constitutional government as a usurper of authority. A local, regional or personal armed band of warriors may refuse to recognize the 'national' unit to which it ostensibly belongs. Sponsorship of military organization may be categorized according to the sponsor's own definition of legitimacy and identity. There are therefore four basic military organizations which each sponsor can distinguish:

(1) Those which are both legitimate and national.
(2) Those which are legitimate and 'sub-national' or local, such as local police forces, which are allied to the national force.
(3) Those which are illegitimate in the eyes of the legal government and yet claim a national identity, such as 'a people's liberation army'.
(4) Those which are illegitimate and 'local', such as the bands of 'thugs' which may be employed by politicians.

These distinctions are crucial to understanding the problems which face the successor state apparatus, especially when it is threatened by rival structures.[2]

After the withdrawal of the colonial presence, the government of an independent state must tackle two principal difficulties in military organization. First, it must attempt to define security according to its own view of the forces at work in society. Second, it must make adjustments in the roles played by public servants in the service of the state. These two priorities of military and security policy form the principal subjects of this chapter.

DEFINITIONS OF SECURITY

What then is the position of the regime which succeeds the colonial power? How does it define the security of the state?

[2] This typology is an adaptation of that used by I. L. Horowitz, *The Three Worlds of Development* (New York: Oxford University Press, 1966), which distinguishes national and regional character, legal and charismatic sanction.

New regimes feel very exposed. The tactics required for opposition to colonial rule required a fairly limited range of activities which the colonial authorities allowed. But independence brought a very wide range of choices. A party organization designed to attack the colonial authority is not necessarily appropriate to manage support for the new regime. The economy is often not strong enough to meet the demands made upon it by the large scale expansion of the state apparatus which follows independence. Most politicians are obliged to lose whatever innocence they had professed in colonial days. Each government has to work out for itself a series of priorities. Which come first, managing support for the regime or making economic decisions to improve the prosperity of the country?

What is the essential difference between the security of the state and the security of the regime? Both state and regime are extremely fragile. The colonial state represented a body of law, however illegitimate; the post-colonial state is a body of men which has captured the state apparatus, buttressed by the sanctions which had been expressed in the final stages of the nationalist struggle. Definitions of security have internal and external aspects. Internal security can only be defined in terms of the system of political competition which has grown up inside the country, often heavily under the influence of the colonial authorities themselves. External security depends on the international environment in which the state was created. The possibilities of external threats are strongly affected by the guarantees which were laid down at the time the new state was recognized in the United Nations. Few African states have had serious external security problems. Somalia in 1960 was a threat to its neighbours because of the large number of Somalis who lived outside its borders. But the homogeneity of Somali culture is exceptional. Paradoxically definitions of internal security are more likely to involve outside powers. The opposition to any regime naturally seeks assistance from abroad. President Nkrumah took advantage of this fact to extend his influence. He began a practice of sheltering governments in exile. Political refugees, whether they were small groups of trained men or large numbers of displaced persons, constituted a peculiar kind of security threat. Uganda, for example, found itself harbouring refugees from the Ruanda revolution, from the Congo disturbances, and from the Sudanese civil war. Subversion against one regime can be planned in the comparative safety of another. When the borders themselves are so imperfectly defined on the ground, the security forces of one state might invade the territory of another in order to capture any opponents of the regime.

In these conditions outside powers, and particularly former colonial authorities, are still very closely concerned with definitions of security. Many states in the former French Community signed agreements with France for the support of their governments in time of emergency. The French army retained its bases in Africa after the granting of independence to the states of French-speaking Africa. The British Government did not retain this degree of responsibility, although it intervened decisively when the East African armies mutinied in 1964. But it still saw the new states as areas of conflict between the major world powers. After the declaration of emergency in Malaya in 1948, the British chiefs of staff had applied an overall formulation of security problems in the colonial empire which concentrated on the cold war. There were three major alternatives – nuclear war, limited war, and the cold war. Colonial authorities were encouraged to prepare for the latter. The new states were warned in similar terms.

Major difficulties face outside powers in the definition of policy when the regimes which were established at independence are overthrown by unconstitutional means. What kind of regime are worthy of recognition? Should overseas aid be reserved for friendly regimes? Important adjustments are necessary when outside powers make themselves primarily responsible for the training of security forces used in new states. It is no longer relevant to train soldiers and policemen to think in cold war terms. Training establishments are obliged to re-plan their courses. Can overseas advisers avoid being identified with a particular regime? New regimes are unlikely to retain advisers who contributed to their predecessors' efficiency. Even such skills as vehicle maintenance or radio communication cannot be regarded as politically neutral.

In many cases, the security of the state cannot in fact be separated from that of the regime, because the main weapon in the armoury of the regime is the state organization itself. Control of the budget and the system of government appointments provides any regime with the means of defeating opponents. The state sometimes appears to be little more than a description which can be applied to those who succeeded to the public offices vacated by colonial administrators. It is regarded primarily as an organization. Its component parts, including the security forces, like all organizations, become subject to political competition. Circumstances encourage all those concerned in 'nation-building' to place a much greater emphasis on the state as an apparatus for government than on the state as a system of law.

In most African societies the rules of customary law, which belong to the traditional authorities of the tribe or the clan, provide the individual with the surest means of redressing a wrong. The institutions which safeguard the ordinary rules of social obligation, such as councils of chiefs, or traditional courts, seem stronger than the institutions which safeguard the state.

Colonial authorities tended to maintain a dual system of law, customary law, which they recognized for petty offences, and the laws of the colony, based upon European models. For example, in British Africa, the criminal law was based on four different brands of codified law. Two were unique to Sierra Leone and Ghana. All the other British territories fell into the other categories, those following the Indian penal code of 1860 and those following a penal code drafted in the Colonial Office based on that of Queensland in 1899. Similarly, the courts followed British procedures of trial, and imposed penal sanctions, such as imprisonment, which was completely alien to the African tradition. The peasantry did not understand the principle of an impartial judge. There is plenty of evidence to suggest that local courts were generally regarded as the arm of the colonial government. When an African in colonial days joined the public service as a soldier or a policeman, he was submitting himself to a discipline based upon European concepts of law. In fact, the disciplined forces of any colonial territory were the first in the public service to recruit Africans in large numbers. Security organizations began with a sense of privilege and a sense of distance from their fellows. In Stanleyville, for example, those recruited by the Belgian authorities for the gendarmerie formed the first regular city-dwellers.

It is not surprising that new states rarely qualify for recognition as legal systems. Professor Hart has described law as the union of primary and secondary rules, and explained that the secondary rules provide the official sanctions of the legal system.[3] Primary rules are derived from the structure of society and its sense of obligation; and are in Africa, therefore, largely the rules of

[3] H. L. A. Hart, *The Concept of Law* (Oxford: Clarendon Press, 1961), Chapter 5.

customary law. These are concerned with all the different ways in which people interact. But secondary rules are on an entirely different level, because they are concerned exclusively with decisions on how primary rules should be interpreted. This task can only be undertaken by a public authority such as the judiciary. African experience of dual systems of law was dominated by the question of finding the appropriate contexts in which to apply European concepts, not with any systematic review of the norms which operated in traditional society. Ironically, expatriate advisers since independence have often been more deeply committed to the codification of customary law than the governments themselves. Those who succeed colonial administrators rarely have a sufficiently common set of values in order to agree about secondary rules. African states can therefore seldom be regarded as legal systems, except, as in Somalia, where all the people within the same boundary enjoy a common cultural inheritance.

The existence of a dual system of law encourages a tendency to think of two different levels of political order, the social order of the local custom and the bureaucratic order of the colonial state. Those with colonial experience find it hard not to think of two separate systems of politics. The achievement of independence in fact brings to the fore the local political system. African politicians have largely been trained in securing the appropriate balance of forces in local affairs, not in the business of 'national' policy-making. The vitality of the nationalist party lies in its ability to secure adequate resources for use by local leaders. The state is regarded primarily as an organization which can provide the means of distribution.

An emphasis on the state as an organization has two important consequences. First, the functions of the state organization are likely to become ends in themselves. Every government has a large number of jobs at its disposal; every government has the job of allocating expenditure between different departments and different regions. Marxist literature has frequently drawn attention to the absence of indigenous entrepreneurs and to the presense of a 'national bourgeoisie', those who enjoy the fruits of office rather than the fruits of capital. The work of Frantz Fanon and of René Dumont have stressed the high proportion of the budget in francophone Africa which is spent on civil servants' salaries. Second, parts of the state organization are likely to develop their own rules, which become more important than the rules of the state itself. When there are no agreed norms on the rules of the game in politics, the discipline which an organization can impose on its members assumes a new significance. The army and the police are naturally the most disciplined parts of the state apparatus. In any crisis they ought to possess the greatest resilience. The army is even stronger than the police. It not only avoids the handicaps of being obliged to deal directly with the public, but is also able to acquire technical assistance from outside to support its actions.

THE STRAINS OF INDEPENDENCE

Can a new state avoid some of the strains of independence? Is it possible to preserve the two different levels of order, the level of custom and the level of the state? The retention of expatriates in key positions of the state apparatus appears to lessen the strain of the first few years of independence. The President of Malawi has declared that he will retain expatriates at the top of his army and his police for many years to come. Such a declaration shows to the rank and file the kind of regime which they are bound to serve.

There are two basic reasons for the strains imposed on security organizations at independence. Both are associated with the peaceful transfer of power by which independence was achieved. First, the new state apparatus is obliged to develop new functions in order to meet the demands made upon it by its fellow states in the international community. Second, the mass of the people inside the boundaries of each new state find for the first time that they have access to the fruits of the state organization *via* their representatives. People expect the government to act on their behalf. These two reasons represent two different sets of problems. How should the state participate in international politics? How should the people identify themselves with the state?

The first reason for strain, the product of international status, is that African experience under colonialism of managing public services was hardly adequate to meet the demands made by the new system. In colonial days, metropolitan organizations provided the overall support for governmental activities in each territory. The sovereignty of the colonial power which defended the juristic existence of the colony also provided staff for its organization. But with the peaceful transfer of power, the juristic existence of a new state was guaranteed by international agreement. Except for the trust territories of Somaliland, Togo, and

Cameroun, the boundaries between existing colonies in tropical Africa were accepted as the basis for international recognition. None of the new states had natural borders, and there were few external security threats. As in many other things, President Nkrumah of Ghana set the example to other states by founding the first external security service with Indian assistance. But other leaders did not give this service such priority. Many Presidents in francophone Africa for example, continued to rely on the French counter-espionage service, SDECE, although the metropolitan power could no longer uphold the state organization unless it were invited to do so.

Those who had been employed to protect the security of the system in conditions of colonial sovereignty found themselves performing similar functions after independence. The army and the police were usually instruments designed by the colonial power. Those joining these organizations had a clear set of roles which were understood by both the colonial authorities and by the people themselves. But the experience of playing these roles was poor preparation for the political conflict to come.

Soldiers and policemen were originally the allies of the colonial authorities which usually divided them into several categories, based on educational attainment. For example, both the British and the French distinguished between those who received regular commission status or regular employment status, and those who were paid simply by the day, or could be dismissed at a moment's notice. An individual's opportunities for gaining the appropriate education, determined the level of entry in the organization to which he might aspire. There were great distinctions in terms of pay and conditions. Responsibility for security in the rural areas of French colonies was divided between the gendarmerie, which maintained higher standards of education, and the irregulars of *suppl'etifs*, who formed the local guard. The latter came directly under the orders of the local district administrator.

The functions of maintaining law and order were therefore carried out by men who belonged closely to the local scene. Such men quickly learnt how to profit from their role as go-betweens for the colonial authorities. They interpreted the white man to the people, and the people to the white man. For example, in Sierra Leone, court messengers and interpreters at the district courts became very powerful local figures. Soldiers, on the other hand, rarely had close contact with their own villages. To be a soldier was to be taken out of one's local context and to be placed under the orders of the colonial power. The difference between soldiers and policemen was even more marked in francophone colonies. Except in Togo and Cameroun, where the League of Nations mandate forbade the use of local soldiers elsewhere, recruits in French-speaking Africa went into the French army, and were therefore liable to be drafted anywhere in the world. The British followed the same practice during World War II. But in normal peacetime conditions soldiers in British colonies came directly under each governor. These distinctions acquired a new significance with the departure of the colonial powers.

Experience gained in serving the colonial governments became something of a handicap under the new nationalist regimes. What did the latter mean to the individual soldier or policeman? First of all, they endangered his notions of a promotional ladder based upon the professional standards of an orthodox career. He now saw two major possibilities. He might now receive either accelerated promotion far beyond his wildest dreams, or he might find his promotion blocked by calculations of politicians. The latter often placed their own kin in key positions, junior officers might be promoted simply because they met the needs of a particular ethnic balance. The time-table of learning responsibility laid down by the colonial authority was quickly abandoned. In the second place, the soldier or policeman saw that new instruments of discipline might be created in order to maintain order. These bodies were a threat to the status of his own organization. For example, many political parties encouraged a militant youth wing. Some in fact gave them drill and provided them with arms. A regime which was sure of the loyalty of the security organization which it had inherited, might well fall back on its own militia. Individual politicians might be tempted to create their own private army from their youngest supporters. Indeed political power was expected to demonstrate itself in this fashion. Successful leaders could incorporate their own private armies into the state apparatus. For example, in 1963 President Houphouet-Boigny of the Ivory Coast created a presidential guard from people living in his own region. The secretary-general of the ruling party at the same time insisted on having his own party militia.

The second reason for strain, the expansion of popular access to government, is perhaps the more important. The colonial authorities limited the opportunities open to the indigenous population, but they provided the chief means of social mobility. The educational systems were largely geared to providing candidates for the public service, and progress up the educational ladder often depending upon the accidents of colonial settlement, or the prejudices of colonial administrators. For example, preference might be given to recruits from particular regions or from particular religious faiths. Areas where Christian missionaries were allowed to work might develop higher educational standards than Muslim areas, as in Nigeria. In recruiting soldiers or policemen, the authorities frequently laid down requirements based upon height, weight or chest measurement. These qualifications, coupled with a certain educational standard, limited the number of possible recruits. The latter came usually from what was described as 'warrior tribes'. Those tribes who had fought the metropolitan armies at the time of colonial conquest were often thought to provide the best guardians of colonial state.

But after independence, all the component parts of the state apparatus were subject to rivalry between different groups. Politicians sought support from their people by ensuring that their own region was represented in the state organization. The colonial authorities have sometimes worked on a quota basis, different proportions from different sources. The new state extended use of this method to include a representation for all groups. It also found it necessary to create new organizations within the state apparatus. The first reason for strain was therefore allied to the second. Any opponents of the new regime failed to get jobs for their supporters. Anyone who had already secured a position in one ministry or department frequently felt obliged to help his kinsmen do the same. The colonial authorities had limited the effects of family obligations in customary society. Popular representations in the new governments gave them a full rein.

The strains experienced by security forces after independence show the true nature of the state which was created by the peaceful transfer of power. Lawyers regard the variety of regimes as different forms of breakdown in the legal order. Professor Hart thinks that studying transfer of power belongs to the pathology of legal systems. He gives three examples of breaks in the legal traditions: (a) rival claims to government; (b) enemy occupation; and (c) anarchy or banditry.[4] The equivalents in the process of decolonization are quite easy to identify. First, the legitimacy of the new regime may be disputed. Second, any new regime may be very vulnerable to outside interference. Third, the state apparatus may collapse through internal strife. The states of tropical Africa therefore share a common problem. How can one

4 H. L. A. Hart, *op. cit.*, pp. 114–15.

create a new legal order, without a revolution, which introduces a completely new conception of the state? Declarations by lawyers on the rule of law for the protection of human rights from the arbitary exercise of power failed to get to grips with the political problems concerned.[5]

Security forces may be able to stand in at an emergency for any breakdown in the legal order, but they usually find it difficult to create a new political order. Their training does not fit them for this function. Armies may claim some legitimacy for their rule when there is a dispute between different factions of politicians. They may also act on behalf of outside powers, or claim to protect the state from outside interference. They can also fill the void if the state apparatus collapses. But the crucial role in creating a new order is the part to be played by the mass of the people. The peaceful transfer of power appeared a legitimate process because large electorates were consulted in giving a mandate to the regimes. Except in the case of the Congo, the people were called on to vote. But there is a great difference between casting a vote and acknowledging that there are limits to violent political action. People who feel that they all belong to the same political order must respect common conventions. The regimes which came to power created their own rules of behaviour.

The colonial authorities maintained a sense of political order because they had the power to limit the political activities of the people. Nationalist parties discovered what levels of activity the authorities would tolerate. Colonial governors seemed to have thought of order in economic terms. They were interested in creating the right conditions in which the indigenous population could be persuaded to work, that is, to give their labour to enterprises brought in by European companies. Although there was a continuous danger of violence, either in towns where the unemployed congregated, or in villages from which forced labour was extracted, the fact that the colonial authorities conceived 'order' in terms of the opportunity which it gives to organize commercial and industrial enterprise, and to protect private property, meant that the colonial regime did not interfere closely with the values of local communities, provided they did not conflict with these objectives.

New states could not act with the same indifference. Much

[5] The Declaration of Dakar on human rights in Africa, was published in the *Bulletin of the International Commission of Jurists*, No. 29, March 1967, pp. 4-17.

more was expected from the new regimes, particularly in terms of economic development. As explained above, the role of the state was regarded in terms of job creation. Young people in particular expected the government to provide them with career prospects. The techniques of man-power planning would hardly be necessary if sufficient capital were available for spontaneous industrial growth. A most remarkable feature of tropical Africa is the large number of young people under the age of fifteen. In the majority of its states over 40 per cent of the population is of school age. This fact alone, coupled with the difficulties of creating a new status apparatus, increases the likelihood of violence.

The circumstances in which these new states were created tended to make their governments hostages to the time-consuming and unproductive business of maintaining internal security. They were placed in the humiliating position of having to divert resources, which could well be employed in enhancing the authority of government, into the task of limiting the consequences of violence from the opposition. The absence of 'civil order' means that those who threaten violence can handicap the work of government.[6] The contexts in which violence might be used are greatly expanded by the diminished authority of new regimes. Either old antagonisms will re-assert themselves, or new organizations, such as the trade unions or the security forces, will be tempted to defend their position by force.[7]

THE SHAPE OF THE CONTEST

It is therefore unrealistic to see the main questions of military and security policy which faced new regimes as if they represented a choice between alternative methods of civilian control. The procedures for limiting independent military action which may be enshrined in Army or Defence Acts, and the disciplinary code promulgated by regulations which are the basis of military law, only make sense in terms of an accepted 'civil order'. The relationship between the state and society is of paramount importance. New regimes are compelled to see military policy as part of the contest with their opponents, whether internal or

[6] Compare, for example, H. Nieburg, 'Uses of Violence', *Journal of Conflict Research*, March 1963, p. 50.

[7] Victor T. LeVine, 'The Course of Political Violence' in W. H. Lewis (editor), *The French-Speaking States of Africa* (New York: Walker, 1965), discusses six categories and devises a typology.

external. The shape of the contest is about the nature of the state. What is legitimate government? What are to be the accepted procedures for conducting public business?

In spite of the preparations made by the colonial authorities for the 'transfer of power', which in some cases produced constitutions of elaborate complexity, each new regime has to fight to impose its interpretation of the answers to these basic questions. Its pronouncements may appear to differ widely from the more orthodox Western concepts of the state. There is inevitably an aggressive 'populist' ring about its declarations of intent, however weak its executive actions. If the regime and its opponents cannot find a common language of communication which avoids the recourse to violence, the actions taken by the executive are unlikely to be the result of consultation. The main feature of government is the official announcement.

At the heart of many African ambitions for the development of a state which will provide the basis of order, is the belief that the methods of consultation used in the 'stateless societies' of pre-colonial Africa can be adapted for modern use. The justification of the 'one-party state' has always contained an element of appealing to past tradition. The notion of 'leadership without élites' retains its appeal. Although each regime inherits an army which is supposed to respond to civilian authority, the ideas of 'civil order' which that regime entertains may have pronounced military features. The political ideals of populist thought confuse distinctions between civil and military. By stressing the need to mobilize the population in support for the regime and in work to improve the wealth of the country, each government attempts to inculcate some of the virtues of military organization.

The presence of armies or other security forces of the colonial type is a handicap to these ambitions. Their chief characteristics, discipline and an effective hierarchy of command were acquired under European systems of government. Military organization with such origins belongs to a context of civil order which is likely to conflict with the conceptions of political achievement of African leaders. What happens to military units which are exposed to an environment in which the legitimacy of government is in question, and the identity of the nation as yet unformed? These features of the transition from colonial rule to independent sovereignty, which have been explained above, dominate the formulation of military policy.

In the political contest which follows the achievement of independence, military units face two alternative dangers. They either face the direct challenge of rival structures, or run the risk of a complete collapse in the structure of command. The first possibility includes a loss of authority caused by the creation of parallel security systems. Policemen are set to watch soldiers; party officials are armed to protect the leadership; people's militia are encouraged to investigate crime. To be displaced by other bodies is a kind of military defeat. The second possibility seems the greatest reversal of professionalism. It is humiliating to discover a mutiny, or to realize that orders will not be obeyed.

The second possibility, the breakdown in command structure explains the wide variety of methods used when the security forces intervene in the political life of new states. The first possibility limits the likelihood of military intervention by setting up other forces of equal capability. An established technique for weakening any potential threat from the army is to build up the police or the militia. If the security forces play some part in the contest over the nature of the state they are more likely to be acting in response to one of the recognizable forms of disruption in the hierarchy of command. There is no African example of the first possibility in its purest form – the successful insurrection carried out by an illegal army which overthrows the legal one – unless it is the armed uprising of January 1964 led by John Okello in Zanzibar. Perhaps the most important examples of the second possibility are those in which a military organization acts in self-defence, in order to try and preserve its coherence.

The different forms which military intervention has taken in West Africa indicate the shape of the contest for establishing a new kind of state. The states concerned all faced considerable economic problems. But while in Upper Volta and Dahomey during 1965–6 there was considerable unrest among the wage-earners of the main towns, the Central African Republic was comparatively calm. In the former, the army undertook the management of the state in response to demands from those in wage employment; in the latter, it acted almost as part of a feud between different branches of the same kin; the President was supported by the gendarmerie and the usurping President, his cousin, by the army. The first *coup* in Nigeria was organized by *ad hoc* groups of officers and men divided into 'assassination squads'; the Ghanaian *coup* of February 1966 was planned at Brigade headquarters in the north, and carried out under the guise of a routine piece of training. The political action taken within the army of Sierra Leone has been at three different levels;

first, by the commander himself who on his own initiative prevented the Governor-General from swearing in a new Prime Minister; second, by the group of senior officers who overthrew their commander in order to establish the National Reformation Council; and third, by the senior warrant officers who renounced the policy pursued by the military rulers.

What combinations of factors are responsible for these differences? The army can only demonstrate its discipline and its effective system of command if it remains united in taking political action. The headquarters staff need to be assured that their orders will be obeyed. With these assurances they can uphold their conception of the state. But in conditions where 'civil order' is poorly defined, military discipline tends to break down. Either specific military units act independently of headquarters, or *ad hoc* groups of soldiers decide to take authority into their own hands. There are thus at least three levels of military intervention: headquarters planning, specific unit action, or armed plotters.

The most important features of the conditions created by the 'peaceful transfer of power' have already been discussed. First, the sponsorship of disciplined forces is conditioned by definitions of legitimate government and of national identity. Only those sponsored by an authority which has the legitimacy of clear national support are assured of a hierarchy of command which will execute orders. Second, the problem of defining security under independent sovereignty draws attention to the exaggerated importance of secondary political activities inside the state apparatus. The role of security forces in the primary activities of law enforcement tends to be neglected. Third, the strain of making adjustments in the roles played by public servants emphasizes the unique position of the security forces. They provide both a point of access for outside powers to express their interests in development, and a means of giving expression to the popular demand for a share in the fruits of office.

The four categories of sponsorship already mentioned can be related to the most significant of the features which have been described. The first two, legitimate organizations on a 'national' or a sub-national level, correspond to the behaviour of security forces which retain their coherence even if they are challenged by rival structures. The second two, illegitimate organizations on a 'national' or 'private army' basis, are similar to the most common products of a breakdown in military discipline, units which act independently of headquarters, and *ad hoc* groups of plotters. Both these types question the legitimacy of established authority and claim a separate identity from the regime in power.

An army which was sponsored by the successor state apparatus on the transfer of power can usually retain its coherence in order to protect civil authority only if it has a sufficient sense of identity with the regime in power. The military regime established in the Sudan in 1958 assumed power with the tacit support of the former civilian Prime Minister because its composition was in character with the predominant political community of the Moslem north. Even if the ethnic composition of the army is profoundly regional, as in Uganda where the Nilotics gained the upper hand, it can easily defend itself against the strains imposed by the nature of political competition if it is readily identifiable with the government. The Uganda army and the Uganda government are closely related.

However, the absence of such a close identity of interest seems the more likely condition for an African military organization. It is often tempted to behave independently of established government, as if it were a 'private army'. It may even be driven to take on the characteristics of a 'liberation movement' dedicated to radical reform. These alternatives, autonomous action and revolutionary support, illustrate the dominant features of the state created by decolonization.

It therefore seems hardly appropriate to treat African armies as if they were the military expressions of an established order. The states which they may be called upon to defend are in many cases extremely vulnerable to outside forces. The interest of the subject does not lie in their fire-power or professional skills, which are of little importance, but in their contribution to the whole process of political development after decolonization. Whenever a few armed men overthrow a government and transform the nature of the regime in power, or whenever the mass of the population remains passive throughout violent engagements between rival structures which compete for control of the state, many questions about the relationship between the state and society go unanswered.

This book explores the implications of the major alternatives facing military organizations created by the departing colonial authorities. Such armies are obliged either to contest the rival claims of other organizations, or to run the risk of internal collapse. If they are faced with a straight contest in civil war, or counter-insurgency operations against rebel movements, they may be tempted to act autonomously almost as a state within a state. If their discipline collapses under the strain of political rivalries, the component parts will form alliances and take political action in support of other groups. The first alternative implies a continued 'military' identity; the second presupposes that other identities are more important. The range of possibilities stem from the fact that the state has not yet achieved that relationship with society which leads to some degree of civil order – a respect for the limitations of violence.

Liberation movements have so far had little success in capturing the states created by decolonization. Although it is a common theme of radical speech-making, the revolutionary war which will bring 'real independence' is difficult to organize. The leader of the Kenya People's Union in his autobiography acknowledges the forces against him, while affirming his faith that only popular support and mobilization will make 'independence' meaningful.[8] By far the most spectacular rival organization to the established state was the people's army which in January 1964 brought revolution to Zanzibar. Its efforts did not involve any 'protracted warfare' and its success was quickly absorbed by Tanzania. The only underground organization which looks capable of establishing 'civil administration' in 'liberated areas' is the 'Partido Africano da Independencia da Guinee Cabo Verde' (PAIGC) which has specialized in the 'protracted warfare' techniques.[9] There are nevertheless ample opportunities for keeping rival organizations hidden. The rebels in Chad, for example, have found an ideal base among the pastoral nomads who live in small communities, a 'ferrick' of seven or eight tents, and who regard all soldiers and policemen as 'natural enemies' preceding the tax-collector.[10]

At the present stage of development in African military affairs, the basic threat of a radical and effective organization to challenge the state is weak enough to justify describing the problems of civil order in terms of the established authorities. What appears at this stage to be distinctive of African military involvement in politics is the army's ability to defend the *status quo*, not against subversion, but against the possibility of break-down caused by the warring factions of those in power. This book must inevitably

[8] Oginga Odinga, *Not Yet Uhuru* (London: Heinemann, 1967), p. 285.
[9] See especially Gerard Chaliand, *Lutte Armée en Afrique* (Paris: Maspero, 1967).
[10] Serge Bromberger, 'Le Tchad, miroir fidèle de toute l'Afrique', *Le Figaro*, 16, March 1967.

C

concentrate upon the fact that the contestants for power do not necessarily use a disciplined form of violence such as that embodied in military organization. The latter can only defeat an enemy which it can identify. The risk of internal collapse, the second possibility, looks therefore more likely than the first, the challenge of rival organizations.

Chapter Two

THE COLONIAL INHERITANCE

THE armies of tropical Africa were largely created from colonial regiments, handed over at the time of independence. The main contrast was between British and French methods. The British regarded local defence forces as the 'national forces' of each territory (see Table Three). This was explicitly stated at the Forces Conference in Lagos in 1953.[1] The French on the other hand, could only create national forces by dividing up existing regiments, according to the origin of their personnel. The 'nationals' of each territory were given the opportunity to return home. This fact alone made it easier for the French to maintain a presence after independence, but it caused great difference in the efficiency of the successor armies. For example, Niger had no officers from the French system to begin its national army while Senegal enjoyed the pick of the best-trained Africans available. There was also a marked contrast between British and French methods of pay. The French Government from its own budget was prepared to pay at full rate all officers serving in Africa after independence. The British encouraged a system by which new states engaged expatriate officers on contract. It meant that whatever the system, African rates of pay stayed somewhere near the European counterparts.

The only exceptions to the British methods of transferring colonial regiments were in Eritrea and Somalia. When the United Nations arranged for the transfer of Eritrea to Ethiopia in 1952, the Eritrean field force, which had been trained originally to fight against Ethiopian bandits, was transferred to the Ethiopian army.[2] Ethiopia fully absorbed Eritrea in 1962. Somalia, at independence in 1960, was created from an amalgamation of British Somaliland and Italian Somaliland. The army was composed of the Somaliland Scouts, originally raised by the British in the north and the gendarmerie originally trained by the Italians in the south. Shortly after this amalgamation, a few officers from the North attempted a *coup d'etat*, but

---

[1] *Report of the West Africa Forces Conference* Col. No. 304, 1954.
[2] G. K. N. Trevaskis, *Eritrea: A Colony on Transition, 1941–52* (London: Oxford University Press, 1960), p. 106.

their plans were foiled by their own N.C.O.s.[3] This appears to be the only case when men from the ranks protected the state against their officers. It demonstrates how exceptional is Somali culture in Africa, where most of the new states had great difficulty in developing a sense of national identity. For example, a common practice in Somalia, the transfer of officers between the police and the army, is rare elsewhere.

What were the most important aspects of this basic pattern to the new regimes? Some tried to avoid taking on the security organizations which they were offered by the colonial powers. The President of Togo, for example, said that he could do without an army. Malawi has always kept its army small, and relied for security purposes on a police force and the party youth wing. Gambia avoided making this decision because the colonial authorities decided to convert the company of troops stationed in Gambia in 1957 into an armed constabulary. How can new states use the instruments which they have been given? A dominant feature of the armies which the colonial powers had created was their divorce from local life. The police forces were more closely engaged with the public as a matter of course, but nearly all the armies had been trained to stand aside. It looked as if the new states could only employ these security organizations in a similar manner to the colonial authorities. The police were the front line of defence, while the army was the ultimate deterrent, only to be used in an emergency.

STRATEGIC VALUE OF COLONIES

The motives of the colonial powers for building large armies were, in the first instance, not directly connected with internal security problems. There were three principal motives. First, the colonies seemed to provide a great reserve of manpower, which could be mobilized in case of war. Second, the possession of colonies gave greater strategic mobility to world powers. Bases in colonies therefore had to be properly protected. Third, all colonial powers were conscious of the need to defend capital investments made by their own nationals, and any mineral rights which had so far not been exploited. This third motive appears to become more important after independence. It is certainly more frequently quoted as a reason for maintaining a military pre-

[3] I. M. Lewis, 'Integration in the Somali Republic', in A. Hazelwood (editor), *African Integration and Disintegration* (London: Oxford University Press, 1967), p. 274.

sence. The French in developing their *force de frappe*, were interested in the protection of those minerals in Africa which are important in the manufacture of atomic weapons. The other two motives were taken seriously throughout the colonial period. The military structures which these considerations produced were naturally separated from local life. Armies were built up in Africa with the prime intention of using them in the interest of the metropolitan power. Any work which they might do within the colony itself was very secondary.

The French were accustomed to looking on black Africa as a source of military manpower. Published histories of colonial regiments list the order of battle for Africans in defence of France in 1914.[4] Nationalist critics of the French Government have always described this system as a mercenary one.[5] British planning in this sphere concentrated on the Indian Army, and on such mercenaries as the Brigade of Gurkhas, whereas the idea of using African forces was not really developed until the Second World War. Several debates of the House of Commons in 1947 on the run-down of colonial troops show that many MPs were concerned to preserve this role for African colonies.[6] The main question at issue was the amount which the War Office was prepared to pay for the privilege of retaining reserves in Africa. The Royal West Africa Frontier Force, for example, was run down after the war to four battalions in Nigeria, two in the Gold Coast, and one in Sierra Leone. All the costing for the maintenance of this force was based on separating internal security roles from reserve roles. The War Office agreed to pay for armies larger than would be needed for internal security, in order to have some base from which to build up a colonial force in a hurry. Normal War Office practice was to distinguish forces required for service with the British Army from forces required for internal security purposes only. Many of the latter had been taken under temporary War Office control during the war. The West African forces and the Cyprus Regiment were those earmarked to provide a nucleus for expansion in case of war.

The strategic advantages of colonies played an important role in British military thinking. The French were less concerned,

[4] *Histoire et Epopée des Troupes Coloniales* (3ème edition, Paris: Les Presses Modernes, 1965), pp. 369 ff., the standard history for the earlier period in nine volumes, *Les Armées Francaises d'Outre-mer* (Paris, 1932), was produced for the 'Exposition Coloniale Internationale de Paris' (Paris, 1931).

[5] Abdoulaye Ly, *Mercenaires Noirs: note sur une forme de l'exploitation des Africains* (Paris: Présence Africaine, 1957).

[6] *H. C. Debates*, Vol. 434, cols. 1652–3, 1954–6, 1689–90, 1963–6.

particularly after the war in Indo-China, with the route to the East; the British, however, for a long time continued to think of Africa in terms of the route to India and the Far East. In the discussions which took place between British and French staff officers at Nairobi in 1950, the dominant theme was the protection of air routes across Africa. The route from Takoradi to Entebbe *via* Kano and the Southern Sudan was very important if either Britain or France was denied air space in North Africa. This route could be used for supplying bases in the Indian Ocean or farther east. At this date the British Chiefs of Staff thought about Africa as a theatre in the next war. It was considered important to keep open not only air routes, but also the land routes between South Africa and Kenya. The Rhodesia Regiment and the Kenya Regiment, both territorials which did not include African troops, were created expressly as reserves of white 'officer material'. White Rhodesians and Kenyans were considered suitable for command in African armies. After 1952, with the revolution in Egypt, and the possibility of an air barrier being created in the Middle East against British aeroplanes, thinking turned to the importance of bases which could be used for a strategic reserve. Although the formation of a strategic reserve was not announced until 1955, and the brigade not designated until 1957,[7] thinking in these terms was already well developed in 1953. This change in strategic thinking made it less important to think of African colonies as reserves of manpower.

INTERNAL SECURITY ROLES

The basic design of British and French forces was therefore to separate internal security roles from the roles of the army. Forces which were intended to act 'on the spot' were used primarily in police work. This design was reflected in the whole history of governmental structure in the colonies. The colonial powers originally had to create a field administration geared both to anticipate and to prevent disorder. The key figure in this system was in English, the District Commissioner, or in French, *le Commandant du Cercle*. These men had the first and primary responsibility for security. There were three levels in the colonial security system. First, the administration collected intelligence, and was primarily concerned with discovering what local people were planning to do. Second, each administrative officer needed

[7] William P. Snyder, *The Politics of British Defence Policy: 1945–1962*, (Columbus: Ohio University Press for Mershon Centre, 1964), p. 12.

a local force which he could call upon in any case of trouble. Each colonial power, therefore, had some kind of mobile force or local force which was at the call of the district officers. Third, if there were a serious emergency, it was necessary to bring in a special force which could intervene. These three roles were common to both the British and French system of colonial government. The Belgian Congo did not quite fit into this pattern. The *Force Publique* was much more of an internal security army than the armies of British and French territories. These three basic levels and roles of action were adapted to British and French constitutional methods. In French-speaking colonies they were completely transformed by the reforms of the French Empire in 1946. These abolished the separate system of justice for Africans, *la justice indigène*, and meant that the French local administrator lost his private army, *les gardes-cercles*. The French security system was remodelled by using the *Gendarmerie d'Outre-mer*. One reason why Africans serving in the French armed forces were even more isolated from local colonial life than those in the British forces was the existence of the gendarmerie. The latter came directly under the Ministry of Defence, and created a special kind of soldier for internal security roles. A decree of 1953 governing the French Empire made it clear that the armed forces were only to be used in a very important emergency. All normal cases would be dealt with by the gendarmerie.

The British design for a security system was governed by two doctrines which held sway in Colonial Office circles. First, until some time in the early 1950s, it was usually argued that the district administrative officer would no longer be required when a colony moved to a certain stage of internal self-government. Second, it was argued that economic development, particularly the growth of towns and the development of trade, required much greater professionalism from the police. These two doctrines were applied to British colonial administration at different speeds, according to the state of politics in each colony. Unlike the French system, which was highly centralized, British colonies did not move together in making their reforms for police and administration. The colonial police in British colonies had always been basically para-military, but from the 1930s onwards, particularly after the work of Dowbiggin in Ceylon, the Inspector General of Police at the Colonial Office instigated changes which moved local colonial forces to a more civilian style.

The need to professionalize the methods used by the police in the discovery of crime meant an increase in the output of African police officers, and higher standards of education throughout the police force. In French-speaking colonies criminal investigation work was primarily confined to the towns, where separate *sûretés* existed. But in English-speaking colonies the criminal investigation department was part of a national police set-up. Moves made in the direction of improving CID work brought to the fore all the tensions which existed within the administration of the colony about the exact role of the police. British advisers attempted to institute a doctrine comparable to that used in Britain itself. This meant regarding the colonial policeman as a constable with his own independent powers of control in law and order. In terms of training, this meant that the police in English-speaking colonies were taught to think of themselves as individual investigators of crime.

But two important factors upset calculations made to further this professionalization. First, the Second World War caused police forces to return more strongly to paramilitary roles, and second, the methods devised by nationalist African movements to harry colonial governments emphasized the rather different social conditions in which colonial forces had to work. Indeed some would argue that without nationalism there would have been no real professionalization of British colonial police. The most obvious feature of the renewed emphasis of paramilitary organization was the development of special units inside the police force for riot control. For example, Uganda created special units in 1942 in the absence of the Uganda Rifles which was then fighting in the Far East.[8] The pressures to reform the police force, and to give it higher professional standards were therefore something more than simply responses to economic change. The effects of nationalism were felt in the early 1950s. The Commissioner of Police in Uganda asked for a special expansion of force in 1953. The Nigerians introduced their special cadet entry system, which was to improve the standards of African officers in the force, by creating a police college course at Ikeja in 1953, and by making special arrangements with the West Riding Constabulary in Britain to run a course at Wakefield for Nigerian students.

The colonial police forces therefore had to face not only increased crime-waves, and an increase in the amount of rioting and violence, but also extremely elaborate arrangements to subvert the state. In British colonial terms, the first experience of

[8] *Habari* (Uganda Police Magazine), March 1964.

subversive movements of any magnitude was in Palestine with the Jewish underground movement. When the British withdrew from Palestine, former Palestine policemen spread themselves throughout the empire. People with experience of Palestine sought employment in many other colonies, just as police officers from India filled vacancies caused by temporary demands (e.g. Egypt, 1953–56). Colonial policemen began to learn new methods of maintaining law and order. In 1950 both MI5 and the Special Branch of Scotland Yard put on a special course for colonial police officers.[9] The commissioners of police for colonial territories, arranged a series of triennial conferences, which began at the Police College in 1951.[10] At these meetings, not only questions of riot control, but also questions of Communist subversion were discussed. Sir Herbert Dowbiggin, a world expert in colonial police matters, spoke to the police college courses in terms which emphasized that methods were nothing, but the training of men was everything. The colonial authorities began to improve the methods used for training their police recruits.

STRUCTURE AND FUNCTION

What was the structure and function of the units created by the colonial authorities for their security forces? In both the British and French tradition, the typical colony depended on three levels of activity for its security. First, the professional army usually stood outside day to day administrative actions; secondly, the police or the gendarmerie, which had special mobile units of intervention, were the mainstay of any government organization in a crisis; and thirdly, each district or each native authority within an indirect rule system employed some kind of local guard or chieftancy police. In spite of the fact that professional reform was against the continuance of this third level, it was still possible to create new local forces if political events required it. For example, after the riots in Sierra Leone in 1955, and the inquiry into violence within the protectorate, it was decided to create a new chieftain police force.

At all three levels on the security system were the guiding hands of expatriate officers. The armies assumed that European

[9] Geoffrey J. Morton, *Just the Job: Some Experiences of Colonial Policemen* (London: Hodder and Stoughton, 1957), p. 273.
[10] *Police College Magazine*, Special Issue 1951, p. 138.

officers and European N.C.O.s were necessary for the 'staff' and administrative work on which all armies depended. For example, in British army parlance, the N.C.O.s in charge of ordnance and quartermastering were usually the most indispensable to any operation. Similarly, the efficiency of the armies was highly dependent on the vehicle mechanics, and the communications and signals men, who were also expatriates. Although professionalization in the police force meant a larger number of African officers, the key posts which were usually last to be Africanized were those concerned with special branch or security intelligence and with radio communication.

The presence of white officers was to some degree responsible for the rivalries which grew up between the armies and the police forces. The police officers were much more committed to their territories. Police work made it necessary to learn local languages, to stay in a country, and to know its traditional forms of behaviour. Criminal investigation is an art only to be practised by those who have some kind of knowledge of local conditions. The profession of arms does not require this kind of skill. Army officers in the British army were therefore usually more remote from the territories in which they served. Although they were expected to learn the language of command if it were not English, there were few sanctions available to a commanding officer to compel them to show real proficiency. Few of those serving in the King's African Rifles (KAR), for example, completed more than a tour of three or six years. Those who remained permanently with the regiment had sometimes failed promotion exams at home. Police officers therefore felt themselves to be superior to their army counterparts, and also felt that they understood the problems of law and order in a way which the army officers did not. To bring the army into security problems was therefore for the police to admit defeat.

Although some of these formal links acquired a new significance after independence, particularly in those states which were ruled by military regimes, official policy towards the army still emphasized its rather separate role. Both the British and the French believed that the key to a good native army was the standards maintained by the N.C.O.s. Both countries expended considerable energy in making sure that suitable recruits came from recognized army families. For example, the French maintained six schools in Africa at key barrack towns, which were designed primarily for the children of serving men. There was considerable competition to enter them. Even in 1956 there were still some 3,000 candidates in the whole of West Africa for the 212 places offered at four schools.

British arrangements were more *ad hoc*. Before the early 1950s some battalions maintained their own schools if they had education officers to spare, and perhaps ran their own boys' companies from which they chose suitable material to enter the main unit of the army. During discussions on improvements which came in the early 1950s, there were several proposals to introduce into Africa the combined cadet force units which were used in British schools. The basic principle in British and French policies was the same. It was to encourage the sons of existing non-commissioned officers to follow in their fathers' footsteps. The British and the French armies recruited for other ranks on a voluntary basis. Each colonial power appears to have accepted certain stereotypes of warrior tribes, which had an aptitude for military life. There was extremely strong competition among the peasantry to enter the army. The army showed itself as a life of comparative privilege.

The majority of units were considered capable of comparatively limited functions. Few armies invested in any expensive weaponry. The basic function was that of an infantry reserve, or even, in some cases, of a pioneer reserve. The men, therefore, had little technical training. Perhaps the most important role was that of training drivers. A large number of men learnt to drive heavy lorries in this way in the army. This fact had some economic importance in those countries which depended upon export crops being transported by road.

When were the armies to be used in internal work? The general tenor of French policy was to discourage the use of the *force armée* for police action. The gendarmerie was considered the appropriate instrument in this field. The most important examples of army intervention in internal security questions come therefore from English-speaking territories. The strike of coal miners in Enugu in Nigeria in 1948 brought home to the colonial authorities the weakness of local police forces. The rifle fire of the police in this instance had been very poorly controlled. But the army was used infrequently. It was called out in Ghana, then the Gold Coast, in 1948. It was also employed during the riots in Sierra Leone in 1955, and also in 1957 when diamond smuggling brought a great increase in security problems.[11] The police

[11] A. Haywood and F. A. S. Clarke, *The History of the Royal West Africa Frontier Force* (Aldershot, England: Gale and Polden, 1964), pp. 475–6, 481.

seemed unable to deal with rural violence. This weakness is not surprising, because their whole training is geared to encouraging the local population to use the judicial process laid down by the state. The army for example had to be brought in to quell the Tiv in Nigeria on several occasions. The revolt of the Bamileke in the Camerouns necessitated a joint operation between British and French forces because of the division of the Camerouns into British and French mandates. The operations on the British side of the border were largely confined to preventing the rebels from escaping and to cutting off their supply lines.

Operations in the Camerouns also indicated how physical conditions affect the concentration and dispersal of security forces. In the conditions found in the Camerouns bush, the most important unit was the platoon and not the company. Indeed in some cases the section under the N.C.O. was the most effective unit in combating guerrilla activity. Wherever the colonial authorities experienced a permanent security threat in the form of local tribal clashes, the structure of the security forces was adapted to meet this kind of danger. The French colonial authorities' campaigns against the Touareg in the French Sudan, or the British operations against the Karamong in Uganda and Kenya, gave the army units a kind of permanent enemy. Such enemies provided the major training exercise.

It is important to understand the psychological impact of military life or police work on the average recruit. The police were obviously not obliged to work as closely together as the soldiers. Their training required them to follow a body of rules in their relationships with the outside world. Soldiers were not so inhibited. The privilege of barrack life encouraged soldiers to think of the army as a state within the state. Before independence in East Africa, many soldiers in the King's African Rifles were heard to refer to the army as their own political party. They regarded the KAR as a more effective organization than KANU, TANU, and UPC.

The well-known authority on French colonial troops, Commandant Chailley, thought that the three kinds of soldier had three different psychological characteristics. First, the regular recruits or conscripts were much closer than the others to traditional society. They did not question the system to which they belonged. Second, the old soldiers, or N.C.O.s, had acquired largely in the process of mixing with Europeans, a whole body of knowledge which was very poorly assimilated. They entertained very unrealistic ideas. Third, the young officer cadets were the best educated. In their minds two systems of values coexisted. They understood the function and purpose of the army in European terms, but they also realized that in their own traditional society they still had certain roles to play. Chailley saw that the young officer cadet found it very difficult indeed to divorce from his military life the roles which were expected from him in his private life.[12] Yet the whole burden of restructuring African armies for independence fell on to this third group. The plans for decolonization were largely about the Africanization of the officer cadre.

PLANS FOR DECOLONIZATION

Although it has no particular significance in the history of police reform, the year 1955 marks a convenient starting point in any study of Africanization in the colonial armies. Between leaving Malaya in 1954 and taking up his post as Chief of the Imperial General Staff in 1955, General Templer was commissioned by a committee of the British Cabinet to write a special report on the future development of colonial local defence forces. This report marked a new stage in British policy-making. At the same time the French army began to evaluate the position about African officers. It began to make special provision for candidates from overseas, usually referred to under the initials R T O M (*Ressortissants des Territoires d'Outre-Mer*). Because the French were working within the unity of a single army, they were able to make a plan for all their French-speaking African territories. In 1956 it was announced that they hoped to produce one African staff officer for every battalion headquarters, one adjutant to the battalion commander in each battalion, one captain for every battalion, and one lieutenant or sub-lieutenant for each company. This meant, in terms of the existing establishment figures, that they were going to create 13 colonels, 20 lieutenant-colonels, 59 *chefs de bataillons*, 142 captains and 172 lieutenants or sub-lieutenants. A crisis had been reached at that stage, because so many of the existing serving officers who were African were due to retire in the near future. There were then 75 African officers, and this figure seemed likely to fall to something like 48 within 10 years if no action was taken. The British, on the other hand, could not act in this co-ordinated way, but General Templer's report instigated a series of negotiations between

[12] M. Chailley, 'Le Soldat Africain' (Centre de Hautes Études d'Administration Musulmane), ronéotypé, No. 3781, 1961.

the War Office and the local commands. It also encouraged the Colonial Office to appoint a special officer, Arthur Majendie, to deal with the planned reforms. To improve the recruitment of officers from Africa into local defence forces, it was necessary to make standing arrangements with the leading British training institutions. The army training section of the War Office negotiated with Sandhurst, other officer cadet schools, and specialist training establishments for certain quotas which could be used by the African commands.

Both the French and the British faced the same problems. First, they both found it difficult to recruit from the best second-ary-educated young men. There was considerable suspicion and indifference to military life among those who had received higher education. For example, the course which the French started in Dakar in 1955 was considered a complete failure because few Africans would come forward for local training.[13] Those who did thought that they really should be sent to France for training comparable with that given to Frenchmen. This sort of complaint in the following year, 1956, led to the establishment of a special school, RTOM, at Fréjus. Partly because of British prejudices, and partly because of the pattern of education in West Africa, the first candidates to come forward for officer training in West Africa came from the northern and poorer parts of their respective colonies. Second, both countries faced the difficulty of bringing African candidates up to their own educational standards within the army. The main purpose of the French course at Fréjus was to bring Africans up to French standards of education in general culture, not simply in military affairs. Similarly, the British had to make special arrangements for extending the length of time given to African officer cadets in order to make sure they could meet the educational requirements of Sandhurst, or the other training establishments which were used, particularly Eaton Hall. Six months was allotted for Africans to have general educa-tional training in the planning of the British programme. This meant that the first candidates to be produced from West Africa spent three and a half years, or sometimes more, in their training.

The French were more conscious of the danger to international peace created by small national armies in a series of new states. They worked to create a single army within the French com-munity, *une armée solide*. In 1955 they appear to have believed that their most important work was to create the right state of

[13] M. Chailley, 'L'Africanization des Cadres de l'Armée', (CHEAM), ronéotypé, No. 2670, 1961.

mind among the new African officer cadre. This meant placing great stress on the unity created by the use of the French language, and by emphasizing the world role which colonial troops could play within the context of the French army. These basic conceptions were changed only by events in the French Community as a whole. After 1959 it was clear that those responsible for training could no longer assume that they were working within a single organization. But they knew that the French army would continue to be stationed in Africa. They therefore made preparations for a situation in which French soldiers would co-operate in manœuvres with the local forces. There was no fundamental change of policy until the decision to reduce French garrisons in Africa in 1964.[14]

The British system meant that the speed of any reform programme depended upon the enthusiasm of the men serving in the field. Each local defence force was ultimately the responsibility of the individual governors of the colonies. The local command structure in West, East and Central Africa was the product of decisions taken during World War II. The General Officer Commanding brought together all the units within his area into a single combatant force, but he was continuously obliged to consult the governors of individual territories. In constitutional terms, the governors were ultimately responsible for local defence forces. Immediately after the war, East Africa Command several times attempted to remove some of the anomalies which arose from this kind of arrangement, but without success. The only method of getting a uniform series of rules was to persuade all the territories to pass the same ordinance through their legislative councils. In spite of the administrative difficulties of running this system, the command structure centralized all questions of ordnance and supply in such a way that local defence forces enjoyed a common system. In terms of reform, the command structure also undertook the prime responsibility for training new African officers. The War Office pattern of communication therefore made it much easier to short circuit the standard Colonial Office methods of work, which involved separate negotiations with each territory. These advantages were preserved in East Africa, even after the War Office had handed over to the colonial governments direct responsibility for the KAR (King's African Rifles). The East African Land Forces Organization, which was created by

[14] This amounted to a reduction of troops from 35,000 to 16,000 and a redeployment. See *Africa Report*, November 1964.

Order in Council in 1957, provided a federal structure for the local armies of Kenya, Uganda and Tanganyika.[15]

World War II not only obliged the War Office to take direct responsibility for African armies, but also gave the latter their first experience of African officers. In the last years of the War, in West Africa, several N.C.O.s were promoted to emergency commissions. In East Africa, a new senior warrant officer class was created to provide a body of African platoon commanders. The granting of the Queen's commission to Africans was therefore already a political issue at the end of the War. Several MPs began asking a series of questions in the House of Commons from 1946 onwards. A decision in principle was taken by the Cabinet in June 1947. If African candidates with sufficiently high educational qualifications came forward, the Army Council was prepared to grant them a commission. However, the implementation of this decision rested upon the local command structure. The local GOC could easily advance or retard development. For example, the Commanding Officer of the Somaliland Scouts found that his enthusiasm for promoting his men was not reciprocated in the headquarters of the Middle East Land Forces. The speed of events in West Africa was due in large measure to the keenness of General Whistler. Before moving to Accra, he had been Commander-in-Chief in the Sudan. Although his appointment to Western Command in the United Kingdom in late 1963 cut short his tour as Commander-in-Chief in West Africa, he was able to instigate a whole series of reforms from 1951 onwards. He took the first steps in planning a series of boys' companies in June 1951, and at the same time made arrangements with training institutions in Britain for the reception of African officer cadets.[16]

But even enthusiastic local commanders faced insuperable legal difficulties in some cases. Soldiers found their proposals being submitted not only to the Colonial Office, but also to the attorney-generals of each territory within the command structure. There were great delays while the legal implications of a particular proposal were worked out. The French Republican tradition avoided comparable problems. After the decision to reform the citizenship laws within the French Empire in 1946, there could be no objection to granting a commission of general

[15] *Correspondence between Secretary of State and East African Governors*, Cmnd. 281; and *Kenya Gazette*, 24 June 1957, Legal Notice 363.
[16] Sir John Smythe, *'Bolo' Whistler: The Life of General Sir Lashmere Whistler: a study in Leadership* (London: Muller, 1967), pp. 198 ff.

statute to a French-speaking African. But until the British Nationality Act of 1948 the inhabitants of British colonies were still divided in terms of citizenship between citizens and protected persons. The latter could not by definition enjoy a Queen's commission. It was proposed several times in the early 1950s to grant special commissions for Africans in the colonial forces under the terms of a special Order in Council. The Army Act of 1955 was eventually used as a means of avoiding these difficulties. General Templer's report on the colonial forces therefore came at an appropriate time. After 1955, Africans were permitted to hold a Queen's commission in the normal manner.

Another legal difficulty which the British experienced was the attempt to limit the powers of African officers over British other ranks. The Army Council in 1948 appears to have decided not to give to African officers the same power of punishment over 'whites' as was possessed by British officers. There was considerable resistance in army circles to giving Africans real officer status. Many thought that the efficiency of these armies still depended upon Europeans being placed in some of the key 'other rank' positions. The most important were orderly room sergeant, regimental and company quartermaster sergeant, signals sergeant, and vehicle mechanic. The British were reluctant to allow African officers to have powers of discipline over these ranks.

The French commitment to a policy of assimilation in Africa prevented them from entertaining such inhibitions, but the numbers of Africans serving in the French army with officer status before the reforms of 1955 were comparatively small. Although the theory of the system made places available to those Africans who had acquired French citizenship, the number able to acquire sufficient education for these positions was limited. In 1950 there were only 66 French African officers, of whom 59 were either lieutenants or sub-lieutenants. At the same date in British Africa, there were only six African officers. What were the effects of British and French efforts in reforming the armies between 1955 and 1960? The great contrast was between the higher echelons. By 1960, the French, through a system of promotion, had ten African staff officers of distinction and experience, four colonels and six *chefs de bataillons*. They had increased the number of African officers from 66 in 1950 to 198 in 1960. But the great majority of these were still very junior, 157 lieutenants or sub-lieutenants. It is difficult to calculate the equivalent numbers in British African territories. But by 1960 about a

D

TABLE THREE

BRITISH COLONIAL BATTALIONS INTO NEW ARMIES
(EAST AND CENTRAL AFRICA)

Batallion No.		*Base*	*New State*

King's African Rifles

3, 5, 11 — in rotation — Nanyuki, Gilgil, Nairobi (Langata) — Kenya

4 — Jinja — Uganda
6 — Dar-es-Salaam (Colito) — Tanganyika
2nd 6 — Tabora — (Tanzania)

1 Nyasa — Zomba — Malawi
2 Nyasa in — Zomba/Ndola
North rotation — Lusaka/Ndola — Zambia
Rhodesia
Regt.

Rhodesia and Nyasaland Army (1954)

Royal Rhodesia Regt. (European territorials) 3 Bn. — Kitwe (disbanded 1964)
2 Bn.* — Bulawayo
1 Bn. — Salisbury

Royal Rhodesian Air Force — Salisbury

Rhodesian Light Infantry (Europeans) — Salisbury

Rhodesian African Rifles (Africans recruited exclusively in SR) — Bulawayo

Rhodesia after U.D.I.

* The SR Battalions were expanded to Battalions 4, 5, and 6.

100 Africans had entered the Royal Military Academy at Sand-hurst (see Table Ten). Of these, about 80 came from either Nigeria or Ghana. At the time of independence therefore, the great majority of African officers in both the English and the French tradition were subalterns of a few years' standing. Those new states which were able to claim the services of the most experienced French officers had great advantages over the rest. The contrast between British and French Africa, therefore, lies in the consequences of two different educational systems. The French divided up their officers corps between the new states they created. The British found that the educational tradition of each colony left its mark.

The presence of European settlers in East and Central Africa had important consequences on the growth of security forces in these areas. As has been said above, the original British policy was to officer 'black' armies with local 'whites'. The Kenya Regiment and Rhodesia Regiment were created with this plan in mind. Therefore in East and Central Africa racial distinctions were much more important than in West Africa. The history of the colonial police underlines this point. In East and Central Africa it was normal to maintain a white inspectorate between the other ranks who were African and the gazetted officers who were expatriate Europeans (see Table Five (*b*)). In West Africa the inspectorate was an African cadre. Plans for the reform of local defence forces found it difficult to avoid the consequences of this colonial legacy.

The Africanization programme presents this contrast in rather stark terms. For example, the local command structure in each area began regular officer training courses at very different dates. West African command began the regular officers special training school at Teshie in the spring of 1953, while East Africa command did not begin its first course until April 1958. In Central Africa the first local course began at Ndola in March 1964. The dates of the first commissions granted to Africans show a similar rate of progress. Nigeria and Ghana had officers in 1947; there were no East Africans at Sandhurst until 1959; the first Zambian was commissioned in 1964. Table Four shows the different rates of Africanization for officers at independence.

It was typical of the contrasts between the political develop-ment of West, East and Central Africa that only East Africa should contemplate the creation of a special cadre which stood below the Queen's commission. Those with Indian Army ex-perience thought that one solution to East African problems would have been the creation of a special commission comparable to the Viceroy's commission in India. Even in 1946 the GOC in East Africa had put forward tentative proposals along those lines, but it was not until April 1953 that General Erskine made the first official moves. The new rank was to be known as GCO (Governor's Commissioned Officer). But the suggestion aroused all kinds of political controversy. The Colonial Office in 1954 said that such a rank would be totally unacceptable to African opinion, unless it could be introduced alongside Queen's commissions. Further delay in reaching a decision was caused by a dispute over the disciplinary powers of officers with a Governor's Commission. The War Office insisted that such officers should not have full powers of disciplinary control over British other ranks. The government of Uganda objected to this proposal, because it already had Europeans working in subordinate roles. The eventual compromise which was announced in the New Year of 1956 after many delays was the availability of the Queen's Commission for East Africans and at the same time the creation of a special rank of warrant officer to be known as *effendi*. The latter was a half-way rank between officers and men. It was defined as a rank suitable for people who were once intended to be officers, but who despite downgrading to the rank of warrant officer retained certain features of commissioned rank. The first course for warrant officers in the KAR suitable for promotion to *effendi* took place in Nairobi in June 1956. The first postings to KAR battalions were in 1957 when eighteen names were gazetted. It is a tribute to the relative autonomy of British officers within this system that even at this stage plans could be sabotaged. For example the officers in the 5th battalion refused to nominate any of their men for promotion to *effendi*, because they were anxious to press for the creation of Queen's commissions. Only one of the *effendis* produced by the first course was posted to this battalion. At the time of Tanganyika's independence in 1961, the KAR battalions had 160 British officers but only 16 Africans, 12 of whom were former *effendi*.[17]

The other startling feature of contrasts in political development was the pre-eminence of the Gold Coast police. None of the police forces in East and Central Africa could maintain the standards laid down by the Gold Coast. The latter, having no 'settlers', had no white inspectorate. When Sir Charles Jeffries wrote his book on the colonial police in 1950 there were only nineteen African gazetted officers in the whole of British Africa.

[17] *The Times*, 27 December, 1961.

Eleven of them were in the Gold Coast.[18] No Ghanaian police officers were sent to the British Police College after 1956. Ghana opened its own Police College in February 1959. At this date the police forces of East Africa had only just begun their process of Africanization in earnest. Between its opening and October 1967 the Ghana Police College trained more than 220 officer cadets on six-month courses. Two special training schools for all three East African territories, one for the CID in 1957, and one for the Special Branch in 1958, were opening as part of this programme.[19] All the plans for the security forces in East Africa were strongly affected by the Mau Mau emergency. The army were not withdrawn from the campaign against the Mau Mau until November 1958. The political atmosphere created by the emergency, coupled with the poorer standards of education found in East Africa, goes a long way towards explaining the contrast between East and West. J. S. Manyo Plange, one of the first Africans in the Gold Coast to be an assistant superintendent of the police, who later moved to Nigeria as a judge, had his appointment gazetted in 1937.[20]

PROSPECTS FOR THE FUTURE

The security forces inherited at independence can therefore only be explained in terms of the colonial experience. What were the most significant differences? It is difficult in retrospect to indicate those features which limited the freedom of action that any new regime could enjoy. There are so many variables to take into account. What kind of state had the peaceful transfer of power created? A most important feature dominating the whole scene was that other powers were interested in gaining a foothold in Africa if the colonial powers did not maintain their predominance. Each new regime had little room for manœuvre in terms of redesigning its security forces. If the colonial power was removed, then other outside powers were necessary in order to support an army. This was less true for the police forces, but even they required arms supplies from outside sources. Similarly, opponents of any new regime were very dependent upon other

[18] Sir Charles Jeffries, *The Colonial Police* (London: Allen & Unwin, 1952), pp. 92–3, 224.

[19] W. Robert Foran, *The Kenya Police: 1887–1960* (London: Robert Hale, 1962), pp. 150, 224.

[20] W. H. Gillespie, *The Gold Coast Police: 1844–1938* (Accra: Government Printer, 1955).

TABLE FOUR (a)

ARMY AFRICANIZATION

(The proportion of commissioned officers at independence)

	Year of independence	Approximate size of army	European or Asian	African	(%) African
Kenya	1963	2,500	85	80	48·5
Uganda	1962	1,000	50	14	21·9
Tanganyika	1961	2,000	58	6	9·4
Malawi	1964	750	40	9	8·4
Zambia	1964	2,200	134	1	0·7
Nigeria	1960	8,000	320	57	15·1
Ghana	1957	7,000	184	27	12·8
Sierra Leone	1961	1,000	50	9	15·2

The column "Commissioned officers" spans European or Asian, African, and (%) African.

TABLE FOUR (b)

POLICE AFRICANIZATION

(The proportion of gazetted officers at independence)

	Year of independence	Approximate size of police force	European or Asian	African	(%) African
Kenya	1963	12,000	180	29	13·9
Uganda	1962	5,400	137	103	42·9
Tanganyika	1961	5,700	189	22	10·4
Malawi	1964	2,600	84	12	12·5
Zambia	1964	5,800	118	18	13·2
Nigeria	1960	12,400	347	88	20·2
Ghana	1957	6,200	71	45	38·8
Sierra Leone	1961	1,800	33	26	44·0

The column "Gazetted officers" spans European or Asian, African, and (%) African.

powers to provide for their armies or liberation movements. The colonial legacy presented a rather stark choice between two alternatives; either the new regime continued to depend upon the former metropolitan power, or it was exposed to the rough winds of international power politics.

The new regimes were naturally suspicious of security organizations which had been hastily put together just before independence. The French army found that the governments of French-speaking states attempted to bully their nationals to join the new armies, although many Africans serving in the French army, wished to retain certain pension rights. The break between the French community and Guinea was symbolized by the total withdrawal of the French in 1958. That country was left to fend for itself. Many Guinean nationals serving in the French army refused to return home. They later became a source of irritation to the French because the Guinean government in retaliation refused to receive them back when they had completed their terms of service in 1964–65. Guinea began with an army of 2,000 men taken from among those who agreed to return.

The most important legacy of the British imperial system in the English-speaking states was the ethnic composition of local defence forces. The British had followed a policy of tribal quotas so closely that hardly any country possessed an army which corresponded to its population. In Nigeria and Ghana, for example, the great majority of the ordinary troops came from the north, and indeed from beyond the northern border of Ghana, while the officer cadre was drawn largely from the southern coastal areas. Each of these local defence forces was therefore conscious of its ethnic composition. Those trained by the French avoided this feeling because they had served in mixed units. The only comparable example in the French empire was the policy in Chad of recruiting from the Negroid south, and not from the Muslim and Arab north. Chadian nationals on their return home from the French army were therefore a rather distinct unit. Only sixty returned from France at independence.[21] The only local forces run by the French were those in Togo and in the Camerouns. Here the terms of the United Nations Mandate prevented them from recruiting men for worldwide service. Togo had a rather similar experience to its neighbour, Ghana. Those who had been recruited into the local force, or into the French army *via* Dahomey usually came from the Northern parts of Togo.

Each new regime began with the assumption that the security

[21] *West Africa*, August 5, 1961.

forces were not necessarily loyal. There is some evidence to suggest that the police and the gendarmerie were more easily assimilable to the new political climate. The nature of police work meant that the nationalist parties had been able to recruit police sympathizers. As has been argued above, the police were less obviously divorced from local life than the army.

The new regimes of tropical Africa were denied the opportunity of exercising the eclecticism shown by Ethiopia. The latter, like Siam in the nineteenth century, having avoided direct administration from a colonial power, could afford to choose from a wide range of possible military advisers. The British reorganized the Ethiopian army in 1944, but since the run-down of the British military mission in the late 1940s, the Emperor of Ethiopia has pursued a policy of great diversity.

Sweden, which had provided a military mission during the 1930s, trained the Ethiopian air force between 1947 and 1958. The Emperor engaged the Norwegians to train his navy; the Israelis to train his parachutists; and the French to train his frogmen. When the new military academy was established at Harar in 1959, it was staffed from India. Addis Ababa became the one capital in Africa with a dense concentration of military attachés. But even this deliberate diversification of military assistance could not avoid the realities of power politics. In practice, the United States replaced the British as the leading power in Ethiopian military circles. Soon after the British military left in 1951, the United States applied to Ethiopia for permission to build a tracking station near Asmara in Eritrea. The chosen site was a perfect one in terms of the orbits used by satellites. A subsequent offer from the United States to give military assistance to Ethiopia was accepted and in 1953 a military adviser group established. This was the most important move made by the United States to establish a base on the African continent after World War II, during which it had enjoyed certain rights in the colonies of West Africa. But America was not closely involved with the growth of the African states until after 1957. When General Lathbury visited Washington in April 1958, on behalf of the British chiefs of staff, he found an extraordinary interest among American officials in the developments which the War Office was promoting in Africa. By 1961–2 the United States had become more deeply involved. Some have argued that the presence of Americans in the aeroplanes alongside the Ethiopian pilots was a decisive factor in enabling the Emperor to defeat the attempted *coup d'état* organized by the

Palace Guard in December 1960.[22] Since that date Ethiopia has certainly been very dependent upon American military aid.

Although Ethiopian policy reminded the new African states of the dangers involved in military assistance programmes, events in Sudan showed the real threat caused by a rebellion in the army. The Sudan was the first new state in Africa to begin its existence with a civil war. It was also the first one to establish a military government less than three years after independence. But in fact the pattern of Sudanese politics does not follow exactly the main lines associated with the peaceful transfer of power. All Sudanese development has been associated with Egypt and with the latter's desire to control the Nile Valley. The army's acceptance of responsibility for government in November 1958 was designed to prevent Egypt taking advantage of the failure to build an effective coalition between the main parties. The Prime Minister, Abdullah Bey Khalil, himself an ex-Brigadier, appears to have agreed to the military take-over. The government which he had formed in 1956 was an unworkable coalition between his own party, the Umma, which was based on the Mahdist sect, and the People's Democratic Party, which was based on the Marghanist Sect, its traditional enemy. He feared that Colonel Nasser would sponsor a national socialist revolution in Khartoum, with the help of the opposition party, the National Unionist Party (NUP). Military rule did not alter the basis of Sudanese politics. It continued to be dominated by the traditional rivalries between the two major religious sects, and between pro-Egyptian and anti-Egyptian forces. After General Abbud had taken power, the composition of the supreme military council, rather than the composition of a coalition government, was the main question at issue. The counter-coups organized by the army during 1959 emphasized this. Muhy el Din, an officer associated with the NUP, led a successful revolt against the supreme council in March, together with Colonel Shennan, but failed in a second attempt to coerce the new government. The mutiny which took place later in the year seems to have been associated with the Peoples Democratic Party.[23]

The leaders of African nationalist movements therefore found

[22] R. Greenfield, *Ethiopia: A New Political History* (London: Pall Mall; New York: Praeger, 1965), p. 422; and cf. Minielier, *The New Republic*, Vol. 145, 21 August, 1961, pp. 15–16.
[23] K. D. D. Henderson, *The Sudan Republic* (London: Benn; New York: Praeger, 1965), Chapter 11.

it difficult to draw any lessons from Sudanese experience, except that involving the civil war in the south. The mutiny of the Equatorial Battalion in 1955 had touched off a secessionist movement in the southern Sudan. But this event was again only explicable in terms of events farther north. The Sudan Defence Force had two features in its history which were not to be found in the armies of tropical Africa. First, it had always been associated with Islam, and indeed treated almost as a great missionary agent on behalf of the Muslim faith. The army originally represented a British sponsored force from the north, based naturally on opponents of the Mahdist Sect. During the period of British rule, both major sects came to be represented inside the army. Secondly, the Defence Force was in fact a kind of federation of local forces. Each of the four corps recruited from a particular region. Three of the corps were from the Islamic areas of the north, and the fourth from the Negroid areas of the south. The latter was in fact created by the British between 1910 and 1919, as part of their policy for protecting the Christians in the south.[24] The mutiny of the Equatorial Battalion and the subsequent secessionist movement were therefore a continuation of southern antipathy to northern infiltration. Dissatisfaction with the government in Khartoum, and disgust for the atrocities committed in its name, seems to have instigated quite a large scale migration out of Equatoria into neighbouring parts of Uganda and the Congo in 1960. When a group of Southerners were finally driven to open revolt, the liberation movement, called 'Anya Nya', was formed in large part from former mutineers in the Sudan Defence Force.

The Mulelist Rebels in the Congo were regarded by the Sudanese government as the natural allies of Anya Nya. It looked as if two secessionist movements had joined together for mutual support. They certainly co-operated in maintaining communications for arms supply. The Sudanese experience therefore became linked with that of the Congo. In both countries rebellion had started through divisions in the security forces. Both countries demonstrated that any rival structures to official security forces needed outside lines of supply. This fact was underlined by the new Sudanese government after the collapse of the military regime in October 1964. Its new policy was to declare itself in favour of the Congolese rebels against the Leopoldville govern-

[24] Robert O. Collins, 'The Sudan Link to the North' in S. Diamond and F. G. Burke (editors) The Transformation of East Africa (New York: Basic Books, 1966), p. 379.

ment under Tshombe and to support the Eritrea Liberation Front against Ethiopia. The latter at the same time faced a war with Somalis living inside its borders in the south-east. This was called the Ogaden Liberation Movement, which was supplied from neighbouring Somalia. Rebellions sustained from outside stood the likeliest chances of success.

All the new states therefore were faced with two major kinds of threat, first, spontaneous internal rebellions which later received aid from outside, and second, subversion actively initiated from outside. The second type was rare and usually ineffective. For example, the subversion carried out in the Camerouns among the Bamileke by the UPC Party (*Union des Populations Camerounaises*), which was actively supported by the Communists through the East German Party, did not succeed in getting away from its regional base. The colonial and independent governments waged war against this movement for a long time. It started in 1951, and was not considered firmly under control until about 1964. The Soviet Union, which gave the UPC moral support, refrained from sending any teams of advisers to visit the country. It relied on Communist party members or other Europeans living on the spot. The Chinese, in contrast, when they began to take a close interest in African events in about 1959, usually agreed to send their own representatives. China was deeply involved in the Congolese rebellion. Work in the neighbouring states of Burundi, and Congo (Brazzaville), was considered subordinate to the essentially dominant theme of Chinese policy, which was to establish a more secure base in the Congo. The doctrines expounded by Mulele were sympathetic to Chinese ears.[25] The Communists have always found it difficult to discover a revolutionary cadre upon which subversion can be built. The Russians tended to despair; the Chinese thought they had found an appropriate instrument in the discontented peasantry of the Congo.

All the new regimes were aware of the ease with which their opponents could secure funds from Communist sources, but it appears to have been difficult to create secret para-military structures unless they were associated with some kind of regional movement. It was easy to secure free military training for one's supporters. Odinga, for example, in Kenya, sent some of his followers to Bulgaria for training. When the authorities refused

[25] R. C. Fox, W. de Craemer, J-M. Ribeaucourt, 'The Second Independence: A cast Study of the Kwilu Rebellion' in *Comparative Studies in History and Society*, VIII (1965–66), especially p. 95.

to absorb them into the armed forces on their return home, they constituted a potential threat. Some politicians claimed that they could create a counter-army to the official structure maintained by the regime.

The peaceful transfer of power, therefore, did not significantly limit the opportunities of other organizations to sponsor other units. The state might in theory have the official monopoly of violence, but in practice a large number of people refuse to surrender their right to rebel. As explained in Chapter I, there were three other major types of sponsor. They were similar to the three alternatives which faced orthodox security forces. First, a unit within the structure of government, for example, a state in a federation, could maintain its own security force under certain constitutional safeguards. The arrangements made to keep such forces subordinate to the national system were similar to those made by any regime which wished to keep the national forces subordinate to its own control. Second, personal armies, or private armies, which had no legitimate status in terms of the orthodox transfer of power, could develop if the state apparatus collapsed. Could any regime prevent its army acting in a similar way? The organization of the army might indeed survive that of the state. Third, representatives of a revolutionary movement from all parts of the country could sponsor a liberation army. This alternative corresponded to revolutionary groups inside the army taking advantage of their position in transforming its role.

These three distinctions are not mutually exclusive. Someone who starts a secessionist movement may change it into something more revolutionary. An army which begins by defending its own interest may finish by creating a revolutionary social situation. But the peculiarities of the peaceful transfer of power seem to have made some possibilities more likely. The very fact that the colonial powers withdrew without a war suggests that the revolutionary situation is difficult to find. Some of the post-independent situations can be explained only in terms of the differences between federal and unitary constitutions devised by the colonial powers.

In the absence of any strong secessionist movement, or open rebellion, security forces may quickly become involved with the defence of their own interests. This role is easier for soldiers to adopt than for policemen. The latter do not enjoy the same privileges. For example, policemen in the Gold Coast were always conscious of the degradation imposed by the colonial system, which meant that policemen were responsible for their own fatigue duty.[26] Gold Coast officers, on the other hand, had batmen to do their domestic work. Similarly, the houses provided in barracks for the officer cadre were usually more impressive than those government houses provided for policemen. In terms of prestige with one's own kin and friends, the position of a military officer was far more likely to carry weight than that of a police officer.

An important consequence of the training provided by colonial powers was the intellectual stimulus of military life, compared with the normal routine of the public service. In the mid-1950s when secondary schoolboys undertook to enter the army, they probably did not realize the excitement which they were likely to meet. Those whose ambition was to enter university tended to despise anyone choosing a military career, but the latter usually attracted people of spirit. The opportunity to go abroad for training, and the stimulus of working out their own problems in strategy or ordnance brought to the fore important qualities of character. The school contempories of these officer cadets probably became either primary school headmasters, or assistants in the public works or health department. They never enjoyed the glamour of service overseas. It was obvious which of these categories represented the state most grandly, and which had the greatest patronage at its disposal. Army officers found it easier to meet the obligations of the extended family system. The colonial training had given them wider horizons, and greater privileges. It is not surprising that the army looked the most resilient part of the state apparatus in any crisis.

[26] The police were successful in getting MPs to put parliamentary questions on their behalf, e.g. *Ghana Parliamentary Debates*, Vol. 19 (1960), col. 238 and Vol. 38 (1965), cols. 940, 1273.

Chapter Three

THE PROBLEMS OF INDEPENDENCE

AFTER the peaceful transfer of power, those who gain public office or hold posts in the public service, are primarily preoccupied with the compelling necessities of creating an effective regime. The situation rarely makes it possible to separate questions of state security from questions of personal power. Where do the security forces stand in post-independence manœuvres?

Forces outside the state have helped to shape two of the most important dimensions of politics. First, the authorities, the bureaucracy, or other organs of state apparatus, are derived directly from colonial models. Second, colonial agreements have largely determined who shall belong to which political community. Only the third dimension, the nature of the regime, is in the hands of local participants alone. How far need security forces be involved in the process of building a regime? The answer to this question obviously depends upon the nature of political competition. Those in power may limit themselves to minor adjustments in the use and deployment of the authorities. But competition may be so fierce that those involved might also be compelled to extend their operations into the community at large.

After the withdrawal of the colonial authorities, the basic struggle for power is to control the levers of the state machine. Many commentators have tried to describe the dominant modes of thinking about the state. Aristide Zolberg, for example, thinks that Africans frequently have a mechanical view of the appropriate means for effecting a policy decision. The state is conceived as a set of levers with which to apply direct pressure on the political community, in order to achieve the government's goals.[1] Some French writers have argued that Africans regard the authorities of the state primarily as sources of personal profit. *L'état, c'est une tartine de beurre.* Can one generalize in this manner? An important feature of the study of security forces is that they are usually the last part of the state apparatus to be exposed to the struggle for power in the new regime. The army is the final symbol of colonial authority. Indeed, in many of the French-

[1] A. R. Zolberg, *Creating Political Order: the Party States of West Africa* (Chicago: Rand McNally, 1966), p. 159.

speaking states, the armies were not in fact handed over to the new regimes until after the date of the formal independence. This fact alone explains why so many of the French-speaking states have been described as French dependants. They have been described as 'téléguidés', bodies which work under radio control from a master transmitter.

Leaders of the new regimes frequently prescribe the role which they would like their security forces to play. Sekou Touré, for example, addresses his soldiers on Army Day each year. The main emphasis of his speeches is the role which the army should play as an extension of the ruling party, the P D G of Guinea.[2] President Kaunda's warnings to the Zambian army are to keep out of political activity. But to study such rhetoric is not a very valuable exercise. What matters is how the security forces act in the process of creating the new regime. The latter is not analogous to a new dynasty, establishing loyal supporters, as was the Egyptian tradition before the 1952 revolution. New regimes are not dynasties, but are a series of competing groups, for which the limits of political action have not yet been determined. The outcome may be the result of a kind of internal war. Violence and threats of violence are constant features on the political scene.

The participation of security forces in the whole business of making a viable regime is extremely difficult to study. There are two points of view. First, soldiers, policemen, and other security officers are obliged to state where they stand in their own local political environment. They are also interested in what they themselves get from the process of competition. The mutiny in Brazzaville in 1966 is a warning to anyone trying to assess the motives for political action taken by the military. This mutiny does not seem to have attempted to overthrow the government, but simply to express disgust with the dismissal of one officer, Captain Ngouabi, from command of the Parachute Commando Battalion. Members of the latter's tribe and mutinous soldiers kidnapped the Chief of Police and the Army Commander and attacked the party headquarters. Each new regime may find that the state's view of the soldier's role may not coincide with that of his own kin, clan or tribe. Much more than simply military status is involved. Secondly, politicians are either viewing the security forces as instruments for the protection of the regime to which they belong, or trying to enlist soldiers or policemen on

[2] Army Day is celebrated in the first week of November, see *Horaya*, the party newspaper, e.g. 7 November, 1961, with special issues on the Army, March 25-27, 1964.

to their own side in some particular dispute. However much the Head of State may define what he thinks security men ought to do, how they act depends on how they are treated by a large number of different interests.

An almost unresearchable aspect of the subject is the magical qualities which seem to surround the exercise of power. Successful leadership in Africa at all levels seems to express itself often in a quasi-military manner. Men have personal followings which behave like private armies. The word 'power' itself has become a symbol to conjure with. It is chanted by Nigerian party groupings; it is drawn on walls; it is shouted at meetings. Political contests derive something of their style from traditional military organization, such as the Asafo companies in Akan society. The destruction of the enemy is carried out by destroying the symbols of his identity, the party flag replacing the household Gods. Young people whose education has removed them from the traditional context may still find magical qualities in the exercise of power. Pierre Erny, after working with youth organizations in Brazzaville, thought that young people had developed a kind of culture of the word, in which spoken words seemed all powerful.[3] The management of words, and endless discussions, were regarded as the key to the social drama in which they were all involved. The abandonment of the roles of traditional society and even of the roles developed during colonial rule can be both stimulating and exciting, but may lead to wholly unrealistic ideas about the management of the state or the structure of the economy.

In a work of this kind, it is only possible to probe into the most obvious features of the political environment. The aim of this chapter is to describe the pattern of military and security policy laid down by independent governments, and to see the initial problems of people working in security organizations when they are obliged to redefine their roles.

The involvement of the great mass of the people in the process of redefinition may be very slight. Professor Vatikiotis in his study of the Egyptian army has shown how the great majority of Arabs regard the state as something alien. They come to terms with the state apparatus, but do not expect to participate in its manœuvres.[4] The peaceful transfer of power in many states of tropical Africa has produced similar feelings. Any sense of civil

[3] P. Erny, 'Parole et travail chez les jeunes d'Afrique Centrale', *Projet*, Septembre–Octobre 1966.

[4] P. J. Vatikiotis, *The Egyptian Army in Politics* (Bloomington, Indiana: Indiana University Press, 1961), pp. 217, 245.

order rests upon the conventions which develop between politicians and people. The part played by the security forces in the creation of any new regime is an important indication of the degree to which political order can be created. Making an effective regime is not necessarily the same as establishing confidence in the political system.

THE AMBIGUITIES OF SUCCESSION

What are the basic alternatives facing a new government when it tries to formulate its security problems? Most governments seem to find great difficulty in thinking out an agreed definition of the national interest. They have to make decisions in two major fields. First, security forces need a supply of weapons, clothing and vehicles. Second, they need some method of testing their capabilities by relating their resources to the wide range of possible threats that have to be met. It may be true that the peaceful transfer of power disguises the accurate definition of such threats. Some are prepared to argue that the international guarantees which preserve the existence of these states make possible the type of political competition which they normally experience in creating new empires or regimes.

It is a great temptation for those outside to prescribe the appropriate methods of nation-building. Many homilies have been delivered against corruption among the new politicians. Others have tried to explain why the growth of a viable system requires the use of what outsiders call bribes, favours or gifts. The British began by teaching a doctrine of public service, which called upon civil servants to abstain from making a personal profit out of their positions. American commentators, with their experience of the party machine in their own domestic politics, have advocated that Africans should pursue a system based on material incentives. David Greenstone, for example, in discussing the local politics of Nairobi and Kampala, thought that the political capacity of the councillors could only be maintained by individual self interest. Given the restricted resources, the political leaders of Kampala could only appeal to the mass of the voters with various symbols; they had to give material pay-offs to the few politicians in charge of the local scene, if they were to create a viable municipal system.[5] Zolberg has argued similarly that

[5] J. D. Greenstone, 'Corruption and Self Interest in Kampala and Nairobi', *Comparative Studies in History & Society*, VIII (1965–6), pp. 199–210.

what Africans need in defining their national interest is not a garrison state, but an arrangement which makes possible a process of constant bargaining. He, like others, has suggested that they should look to the political machine in the United States for a model of behaviour.[6]

Whatever the influence of the peaceful transfer of power, the political competition found in new states shares certain common features. Two are predominant. First, leaders find that they can only control their followers through some patronage or clientage system, which develops its own rules of social obligation. Leaders secure places of profit, contracts, or more extensive resources for their followers, who in return demonstrate their support. Martin Kilson has described competition in Sierra Leone in terms of 'the principle of reciprocity.' He argues that the exchange of gifts binds an individual to his unit, and that these loyalties can be seen in operation while the coalitions which form a government are being made.

Such loyalties within any coalition maintain certain sub-identities which major difficulties bring into the open.[7] This kind of argument applies to the behaviour of the security forces as much as to other groups in society, if there is a system of extensive competition. One must expect to find certain sub-identities inside an army or a police force which might be more important in certain crises than traditional norms or organizational discipline.

The second feature of political competition which seems common to African states is that any leader requires his own intelligence system. If loyalties are only maintained by material incentives, than each person in a contest needs to know how rapidly allegiances might change. The development of security forces after independence betrays this feature in a very obvious way. Most regimes find it necessary to provide themselves with some other source of information than the official channels of military intelligence or special branch police. In other words, the security forces alone cannot be relied upon. Their allegiance is naturally in question, not because they are natural enemies of any regime, but because the allegiance of everybody is open to question.

Apart from these two features of political competition which

---

[6] Zolberg, op. cit., pp. 158–60.

[7] Martin Kilson, *Political Change in a West African State: a study of the modernization process in Sierra Leone* (Cambridge, Massachusetts: Harvard University Press, 1966), pp. 268, 270, 274–5, 278.

characterize internal politics, these are additional complications as a result of external factors. For example, a new regime may act as host to the dissidents of other regimes in neighbouring states. Nkrumah in Ghana gave strong support to the opposition parties in Niger, Togo, and the Camerouns. Tanzania has for a long time been host to the liberation movements fighting the Portuguese in Mozambique. The Leopoldville regime in the Democratic Republic of the Congo experienced such difficulties from fights between opposing factions in the Angola Liberation Movement that it was compelled to ban one party. Zambia now faces similar difficulties in its protection of freedom fighters working in Rhodesia and Southern Africa. The presence of such movements may cause an expansion of security forces beyond immediate needs. Regimes which find opponents on the other side of international boundaries may be tempted to retaliate. The Ethiopian police are believed to have arranged the assassination of the leaders of the Eritrean Liberation Front who had sought shelter in Khartoum. But most main regimes find it difficult to infiltrate their agents into another system. Malawi has not found it possible to destroy the army raised by Mr Chipembere which is based on Tanzania.

When political competition is of this nature, and security threats of this order, how does a regime define its security problems? One can only begin with those regimes which have not collapsed immediately after independence. As Zolberg (see p. 6n) has pointed out, the Democratic Republic of the Congo experienced all the strains of the transfer of power at a single moment in time, while other states have felt them at different degrees and on different time scales. If anarchy is such that the state apparatus can no longer control those who lie within its internationally recognized political community, the regime has no real choice in defining its security policy. Rebuilding the state and defining security problems amount to the same thing. After the failure of the UN to reconstruct the Congolese army, Prime Minister Adoula in April 1963 was obliged to renegotiate for Belgian military assistance. The reconstruction of the regime called for an injection of colonialist efficiency.

But what has happened in the majority of cases where the state apparatus has not collapsed? Each new regime enjoys a certain degree of choice in the two basic fields of policy, supply and efficient administration. Most of the decisions which have been taken have been based on the exigencies of the moment. Military policy takes its colour and tone from the evolution of the difficulties encountered in establishing authority, when the majority of regimes are highly personal organizations.

The first area of choice, supply, will be dealt with in greater detail in the next chapter, but the effectiveness of a regime cannot be divorced from it. Each regime has to come to terms with the former metropolitan powers. It has to decide how far it is going to be dependent for the maintenance of the security system. The weapons, uniforms, and vehicles in use are all on the former colonial pattern. The language of command, and the system of training follow that of the former metropolitan power. The latter rarely designed its system of supply on a territorial basis. European ministers of defence were accustomed to think on a continental scale, and the construction of bases was related to their strategy, not to the boundaries of colonial territories. The Central African Republic had to look for its supplies either to the French base in the north at Fort Lamy or to Brazzaville in the south. Malawi depended for its military supplies on the barracks in Rhodesia. Uganda called on the East Africa command structure in Nairobi if it had any difficulties.

How far could this inter-territorial co-operation be continued into the post-independence world? Nkrumah thought that a Pan-African command structure would eliminate dependence on the former colonial powers, but he was opposed, frequently and bitterly, by those who thought that he was attempting to place Ghana at the centre of African military strategy. There appear to have been few real attempts at co-operation after independence, although there are several examples in British Africa of co-operation between independent states and colonies. Nigeria continued to send officers for training at Teshie in Ghana between 1956 and 1960. Uganda still looked for maintenance to Nairobi during 1962–63, but when Tanganyika in February 1963 proposed to the Uganda government a scheme for military co-operation, it was not well received. Such a plan did not seem immediately relevant to the problems of political competition in Uganda. The latter therefore compromised with a treaty of military assistance, which avoided serious commitment.

Not surprisingly, those who had the most to gain from some kind of international co-operation within Africa were those who had made an irrevocable decision to break with the former colonial power. It might be argued that Guinea's rejection of General de Gaulle's offer in 1958, and Mali's decision to break with the French community in 1961, after the collapse of its federation with Senegal, constituted actions which lay outside the normal procedures of the peaceful transfer of power. The rupture was violent. The French are alleged to have burnt equipment rather than hand it over to the Guineans. The President of Mali in his first order of the day to the new army praised the party's decision to negotiate for the evacuation of French bases. But in making a clean break with the past, both Guinea and Mali knew that they were placing themselves under another form of dependence, Guinea with Russia and Mali with the United States. Elsewhere, the process of breaking with the colonial power has usually been more gradual. The reasons for exercising this choice are not always immediately apparent. Nor are the consequences of the break necessarily premeditated.

The closer an army stays to its metropolitan sources of supply, the more it tends to think of itself as an autonomous organization. Soldiers are not really obliged to adjust their behaviour to the post-independent situation if they continue to work with expatriate officers. In contrast, policemen have to be more flexible. The police force cannot enjoy the kind of status which is given to the army by its independent source of supply, for policemen do not need any complicated weapons. The francophone states are more fully committed to the French presence than the anglophone to the British. The defence agreements which France signed with its former colonies, appeared to make the new national armies into allies of the French army. The latter was available to intervene in co-operation with the local army if there were any cases of severe disorder. Only the Camerouns qualified the defence agreement which they signed with France. Even Congo (Brazzaville) retained French officers in the military school, *Ecole Leclerc*, when it was decided to weaken the national army by removing its French support.

In the anglophone states, the army found it difficult to act independently of the state apparatus. Although the British on their withdrawal did not insist on important defence agreements, they nevertheless hoped that the local forces would continue to enjoy British aid. The anglophone regimes sometimes found the presence of British officers an embarrassment. Ghana established a precedent in 1961 when Nkrumah dismissed General Alexander. The British were considered a handicap to Nkrumah's plans for using the Ghanaian army in strengthening his foreign policy. Similarly, the refusal of the Presidents of Tanzania and Uganda in the spring of 1964 to accept a British training mission, stemmed from their conviction that British officers were not

sympathetic with the important political role which they themselves expected their armies to play. The mutinies which took
place in three East African armies in January 1964 provided an
excellent excuse for realignment. The Nigerian position was more
complex. The federal system hindered the development of a
clear role for the army. The Federal Ministry of Defence was not
as enthusiastic for co-operation with Britain as the army itself.
The breach in diplomatic relations between Britain and Somalia
was entirely due to British policy for the northern frontier district
in Kenya. British relations with the Somalis were dominated by
Somali claims to parts of Ethiopia.

Although there seemed to be more deviants from loyalty to the
mother country among anglophone states than among francophone, the majority of new regimes established in tropical Africa
were prepared to depend upon the metropolitan power for their
sources of military supply. The environment created by this dependence relationship, as has been explained above, was partly
responsible for the kind of political competition which determined the future. Most of these states in the years immediately
before their independence had been dominated by a contest
for power which the colonial authorities had attempted to
regulate.

The second area of security policy in which each new regime
was able to make a choice was the efficient design of military
units or para-military organizations. If the security problems of
the new state could be accurately defined, then plans could be
made for creating the most appropriate units to meet them.
Absolute efficiency required some degree of mobility. For instance, the presence of guerrilla bands required a more widely
dispersed professional army. Infiltration across the borders by
bandits meant training an adequate frontier guard. Could not
most of the new states have relied on some kind of armed constabulary? If they were not under any serious external threat,
could they not depend upon a small professional army with
perhaps a large reserve? The range of choices in this field reflects
the real dilemma of each new regime. Considerations of efficiency
may in fact be a blow to a national pride or sheer political naïvete.
No regime could re-design security units on functional grounds
alone.

The presence of expatriate officers sometimes underlined this
dilemma. For example, the British officers working in Kenya
argued against any great expansion of the Kenyan army, because
they considered aid from outside would always be forthcoming

if there were a serious threat of invasion from Somalia. Kenya could rely on its alliance with Ethiopia and upon its connections with Britain. But for the Kenyan Government to admit the force of this argument, it had to confess that there were other motives for expansion. The regime feared the machinations of its opponents in the Kenya People's Union. When security is defined according to the fears of the regime, and not according to the arguments of efficiency, it is difficult to say what relationship the design of military units has to the real threats which they might face.

The central fact of political competition in new states is that the traditional expressions of loyalty to a leader bear strong resemblances to the obligations of military service. The easiest way of translating the colonial set of obligations between officers and men into post-colonial terms is to look at military units as if they were political support organizations. The expansion of the new armies and the design of new units within them may therefore be strongly influenced by the political demands made by those promising to support a new regime. Once again, the police forces are not so vulnerable as the armies to this kind of re-organization. It was symptomatic of the new regimes which were being established that political leaders should address themselves to the men rather than to the officers and N.C.O.s. The latter seemed much more likely to be anxious to maintain colonial procedures.

There were therefore serious ambiguities in the security policies of the regimes established by the transfer of power. In the first place, when considering the dependence of the new armies on metropolitan sources of supply, security forces were tempted to see the aid which they received as an additional political resource to strengthen the army. That is why it was quite easy for the regime to regard the army as an expression of outside interference, or indeed as the continuation of colonial power. In the second place, any attempt to make the design of military units seem more appropriate to the needs of a developing country ran into obstacles raised by the way politics was conducted, which seemed more important than the real threats to the security of the state. Indeed the latter could not easily be identified. Each of the areas in which a new regime had the opportunity to make decisions for the transformation of its security forces contains a considerable risk. There are two major alternatives: either the security forces behave in an autonomous manner and in fact make little adjustment to the new political situation, or the fierceness of political competition and their involvement in it, overwhelms the coherence of their original command structure. These two dangers were discussed in the first chapter. They represent almost structural weaknesses in the process known as the transfer of power.

The next two chapters discuss some of the ways in which these dangers are faced. Can a new regime teach new roles to its soldiers or policemen? Can it prevent the people falling under its jurisdiction from spending inordinate amounts of time and energy in seeking political rewards from the new system? If the members of the security forces acquire some kind of national ethic, they are less likely to behave independently of the state. If the allocation of resources is not solely by intrigue and inclination, the discipline of the security forces may not be overwhelmed. But there are strong vested interests in the combination of colonial roles and traditional roles. French commentators have emphasized how much each new state can be closely identified with the ruling class, la classe dirigeante, which consists almost entirely of state functionaries and the employees of expatriate enterprises. Jules Gérard-Libois thinks that the Congolese state can be identified with about 300,000 people who in various capacities were the beneficiaries of the colonial regime.[8] Traditional methods of rewarding political service are perhaps more important in making it difficult to set limits around political action. Holding office gives one the right to eat its fruits. Many African proverbs, and indeed the words used to describe the exercise of power, are associated with the idea of personal consumption of food. To create a new regime is to exploit traditional methods of bargaining and rewarding as well as to maintain the bureaucracy created by the colonial power.

What happens, then, to the roles learnt under colonial sovereignty as soon as the metropolitan power has withdrawn its representatives? The degree to which security forces learn to adjust themselves seems to depend on their standing within the new regime which is being created. The army is affected by the nature of politics; even while the state apparatus remains intact, if the strains laid on the latter become too strong, it may find itself intervening and taking over the political process itself.

[8] 'The New Class and Rebellion in the Congo' in R. Miliband and J. Saville (editors) The Socialist Register (London: Merlin Press, 1966), pp. 267–80.

INTELLIGENCE AND SECURITY

To look more closely at the two fields which have been already defined, the supply of material and the design of efficient units, it is necessary to relate them to the two features of political competition outlined above. The second feature, the development of private intelligence systems by the political supporters, corresponds more closely than the first feature to conditions of colonial power. The first feature, the management of political support through some sort of clientage or patronage system, is more closely connected with the political methods of traditional society.

One of the prime functions of the state apparatus in colonial days was to maintain a comprehensive intelligence system on all important individuals. The administrative officer in the district for which he had responsibility, was trained to look for the tell-tale signs of conspiracy, or of possible outbreaks of rural violence. The District Commissioner was the lynch-pin in providing the colonial government with an accurate forecast of internal security threats. As the colonial police, in British Africa at least, became more professional, the policemen performed this function. Particularly throughout the period during 1950s when nationalist parties were beginning their activities, the authorities in British Africa learnt about challenges to their rule through an established committee system at district and provincial level.

President Nkrumah, for example, in Ghana continued to use the British intelligence committee structure. He merely took the place of the Governor on the Central Intelligence Committee, and as the Governor had done, received the reports of Assistant Commissioner (Special Branch). The Central Committee and also the regional committees contained representatives of the army, the Ministry of Labour and the Ministry of Local Government or the Interior. It was normal throughout British Africa to find labour officers and secretaries of local councils as well as Special Branch policemen and intelligence officers in the army associated with this structure. The army commander, and perhaps the director of intelligence for the local army, was the principal link between the regime which received this information and the security forces which were to act on it. Sometimes expatriate officers continued to hold key positions. For example, although the British Assistant Commissioner (Special Branch) in Ghana resigned in 1959, he remained as special adviser until

1962. A change of political atmosphere can easily be detected if expatriate officers are removed from this committee structure. There are again some marked contrasts between anglophone and francophone countries in this respect. The secretariats maintained by several French-speaking Presidents retained Frenchmen in the key espionage roles. The British usually learned the weakness of their position when expatriate officers are removed from position of confidence. For example, almost two months before the mutiny, Brigadier Douglas, the Tanganyikan army commander, was removed from the intelligence committee in November 1963. This was a sign that even if the mutiny had not taken place, the British presence was no longer really welcomed.

What is the effect of post-independence politics on the different aspects of security. There seem to be two main features, both of which are associated with the second field of policy choice, namely the design of military units. Africans have been most resourceful in finding out new ways of extracting political information. First, the intelligence system designed by the colonial power tends to become highly personalized, particularly around the Head of State. Sometimes it looks as if each political leader is attempting to create his own system. Second, the nature of fierce rivalry for the fruits of office encourages the development of parallel systems of espionage. Nobody can trust a single course of information, unless it has been checked by another authority. All African politicians have to learn the art of identifying the difference between effective challenges to their position and verbal abuse. The principal weapon of African politics is personal intimidation. Asking for the dissolution of the Uganda Parliament with almost Cromwellian vehemence, Abu Mayanja summarized his position with the telling phrase: 'We all of us here intimidate each other.'[9] Precisely because of its importance, the transformation of the methods used for internal security after independence is extremely difficult to study. All espionage systems depend upon cut-off points to prevent the enemy knowing the origin of any information which may be intercepted.

The day-to-day functions of the police are such that they cannot avoid being involved in any adjustments of the intelligence system. The army may be able to remain aloof, especially if it can continue to play a kind of mercenary role. But the police are required both to report on individuals, and to enforce the law. They may well meet with the hostility of politicians, or with

[9] *Uganda National Assembly Debates*, Vol. 61, p. 241.

public servants in the process of law enforcement, particularly if they attempt to continue an expression of the legal norms defined by the expatriate colonial power. Politicians in an independent state expect to be able to bend the rules laid down by the departing colonial power, particularly in such fields as public finance and appointment to office. Policemen therefore have to come to terms with whatever regime establishes itself in power. Their intelligence functions can be quite easily placed at the disposal of their new masters.

A good indication of the change in political atmosphere which follows independence is the fate of the special branch of the police. In British Africa at any rate, this branch has been kept relatively small by the colonial power. A contrast of regimes is presented by the differences between those which permit it to continue, as an accepted method of tracing subversion, and those which remove it from police control. The Head of State in a new regime may require the special branch to become a personal service. For example, President Kaunda turned the Zambian special branch in August 1967 into a civilian organization. If it remains under police control, it may nevertheless be colonized by political influences. A formerly influential minister in the Obote Cabinet in Uganda, Nekyon, placed his brother-in-law, Odongo, in the seat of the Head of Special Branch. Prime Minister Obote himself transformed the post of Head of Protocol into an intelligence bureau. He placed in it his nephew, Adena Adoko. Members of Parliament amused themselves by asking questions about the movements of the Head of Protocol. He was known to manage a system which had representative informants in each district office.

The most extreme example of a break in relations between the police and a particular regime was that which took place in Ghana. After the attempt on his life in August 1962, at Kulungugu, President Nkrumah felt that he could no longer trust the special branch system. He decided to institute a new national security service in 1963. This necessitated the transfer of Special Branch officers from the police force into a new system directly under the President's control. He placed at the head of it a member of his own tribe, Ambrose Yankey, who had been chosen by the retiring expatriate Commissioner of Police largely on the basis of this ethnic [qualification. These moves were made to humiliate the Ghanaian police force. The latter was in fact purged of its top officer cadre in January 1964 after what appeared to be a police plot to assassinate the President.

Commissioner Amaning was accused of posting a police constable in Flagstaff House, the President's mansion, with strict orders to kill the President. He only succeeded in killing one of the latter's bodyguards. It was in fact this purge of the officer cadre which brought Mr Harlley to the post of Commissioner, although he was kept in an acting rank position for a considerable time.

An interesting aspect of this Ghanaian incident was that Commissioner Harlley appears to have retained his own intelligence system inside the uniform branch of the police. Some people allege that he had already made up his mind to remove Nkrumah from power before the previous assassination attempt. He was certainly very prominent in planning the *coup* of February 1966. The uniform branch, which Harlley commanded, was deliberately kept in an inferior position to the National Security Service. For example, a sergeant in the latter, if he transferred from the police force, was likely to almost double his monthly pay.

Wherever the Special Branch is transformed into a private and almost personal security service for the Head of State, he may still find it necessary to use his own political party as an alternative source of intelligence. His private policemen can always be checked by his party spies. This phenomenon is known in a wide variety of African parties. President Banda in Malawi finds it useful to encourage the Womens' Congress section of the party to provide him with political information. President Senghor in Senegal maintains a very extensive network of correspondents in the *Union Progressiste Senegalaise*. Even where the party is modelled more closely on Leninist lines, it is not unusual to find private protection systems within the official party system. The 'Chinese Faction' within the *Union Soudanaise* in Mali seems to have had a highly organized series of informants. It is alleged that Mamadou Gologo, who as Minister of Information was officially responsible for counter-espionage work, also ran his own spy system. But accurate information on these methods of maintaining a system of loyalty is very hard to discover. The military regime in Ghana has published the most extensive account of the system run on behalf of President Nkrumah.

The army, unlike the police, does not often become an instrument in this kind of political manœuvre. It is usually in the position of being spied upon rather than of spying. Mali, Guinea, and Tanzania are the only countries in tropical Africa which are known to have developed a political commissar structure inside their armies. Wherever such a system is introduced, it marks a natural break with the hierarchy of command which the colonial authorities understood. An established local defence force, with expatriate officers, would tend to resist its introduction. Because Mali and Guinea began their military reconstruction after a total break in relations with France, they were able to establish political control over the army from the very beginning. Guinea has extended its system by developing a peoples' army militia, but this design of a military unit still remains the exception rather than the rule.

Again Ghana provides the best example of an attempt by a new regime to impose political control on a colonial-type army. When he decided to break relations with Britain in military training, and to introduce Ghanaians throughout the army, President Nkrumah determined that he would reform the system of military intelligence. In 1961 he took Hassan out of the diplomatic service, promoted him to Lieutenant Colonel, and appointed him as Director of Military Intelligence. As Brigadier Afrifa has shown in his book on the Ghana coup, this appointment aroused considerable resentment in the army.[10] Hassan was trusted and respected by Nkrumah. They belonged to the same tribe, although the former had been converted to Islam and had spent considerable time in Khartoum, where he organized the office for pilgrims crossing from Nigeria to Mecca. Hassan's appointment as head of Military intelligence meant the introduction of informants into the army linked with the National Security Service system. The officer corps were made conscious that they were under surveillance. Each man became careful to guard his remarks in front of strangers. Even the Commandant of the Military Training College, Colonel Sanni-Thomas, became subject to suspicion simply because he was related to the President by marriage.

Nkrumah's desire for a highly personal system was reflected in his use of his own tribesmen. Not only Colonel Hassan, but also Ambrose Yankey, his son, and Ben Farjoe, who operated in the highest organs of the National Security Service, were Nzima. The latter come from the south-west of Ghana. The predominance of northerners in the army, and the presence of large numbers of Ewe in technical jobs, gave the conflict between the army and the security system a tribal flavour.

But the basis of Nkrumah's system was to create a kind of counter army, recruited from the ranks of the existing battalions.

[10] A. A. Afrifa, *The Ghana Coup* (London: Frank Cass, 1966), pp. 100–2.

The arrangements made for a company to guard the President's palace were extended in 1962 to include a whole regiment. In the year before the *coup* a second regiment was being established. The guard belonged to a section of the National Security Service known as the 'Presidential Detail Department'. These regiments were of battalion strength and were composed of Ghanaian soldiers who volunteered or were detailed to join this service. Colonel Zanlerigu, their Commanding Officer, was aided by Russian and East German advisers. Those in the army who were not detailed to guard the President were, as in the case of the policemen, deliberately humiliated. They were left without new equipment or new uniforms, while those in the Presidential Guard received the best in any fresh supply. The soldier most loyal to the President, General Barwah, was entrusted with the key position in the National Security Service, from which he could supervise not only military intelligence questions, and the development of the presidential guard, but also the training of freedom fighters for other African countries on Ghanaian soil. When the *coup* came in February 1966, the plot was based upon the brigade stationed in the north at Tamale. As a military operation, it looked like a small civil war inside the army, as if the periphery had attacked the centre, or the subordinate units their own headquarters. Those who happened to be defending Flagstaff House on behalf of the President at the time had not been hand-picked for reasons of any political loyalty. As Northerners predominated, it was Northern soldiers against Northern soldiers, commanded by officers with different political loyalties.

Both the officer corps of the police and of the army in Ghana found the Nkrumah security system a threat to the tradition of discipline in which they had been educated. Both were highly influenced by British methods. They resented the fact that their subordinates might be employed as informants on behalf of the National Security Service. The Director of Music in the police was detained without any explanation being given when he attempted to discipline one of his own bandsmen. This type of incident caused grave offence.

The Ghanaian National Security Service of 1963 illustrates how far the colonial system can be transformed without actually moving over to a fully totalitarian structure of state police. Nkrumah was not in fact sufficiently ruthless to be successful in his reconstruction of the security forces. The conventions of Ghanaian society was inhibiting. The President himself seemed reluctant to shed blood, and the methods of intimidation depended chiefly on the Preventive Detention Act under which opponents could be arrested without trial. The chief fear of all Ghanaians during this period was that of being put 'inside'. Furthermore, those who had responsibility for maintaining state security were not in fact disciplined in any real ideology. The attempt to impose Nkrumahism was a dismal failure. Although the President ordered army officers to attend the party ideological institute at Winneba, it was quite easy for them to find excuses not to go. All army officers in 1963 were in fact obliged to join the ruling party, the Convention People's Party (CPP), and all agreed to do so though with varying degrees of cynicism. By the summer of 1965, the President suspected that he had pushed the officer corps too far. He dismissed Generals Otu and Ankrah, and there is evidence to suggest that he knew the arrangements which he had made, in giving charge of one of the brigades to Colonel Kotoka, could only be temporary. The regime was in danger as soon as one of the brigades came under the command of an officer who was likely to defend the army's honour. Kotoka was one of the few men who had the guts to carry out what so many of the others desired to see.

Just as Ghanaian officers appeared to cling to British laws, so Ghanaian judges were regarded by the regime as too closely wedded to the British legal system after independence. There was a continuous temptation for the new leaders to defend their regime by an appeal to popular justice. There have been various experiments in peoples' courts in terms of the philosophy of the new states; many argue that indigenous judicial concepts can be used to replace the legal system of the colonial power and to find procedures and sanctions more acceptable to the new regime. The basic problem is how to redefine crime, procedures, and sanctions. Why is it that so little energy has been put into the cause of legal reform? Ironically, expatriate advisers have sometimes been the most enthusiastic in forcing the pace of legal adjustments.

Those Ghanaian judges who disliked the general trend of Nkrumah's regime were placed under great pressure, even from their own colleagues. Tension between the judiciary and the regime came to a point of crisis in December 1963 when the President dismissed the Supreme Court Judge. After the state trial in which three who were accused of subversion were exonerated, the judiciary no longer appeared to respect the laws which Parliament made, and which the constitution required them to interpret. Several judges resented bitterly the consequences of the dismissal of the Chief Justice. Under the new arrangements for state trials introduced in 1964, the British tradition that an accused person should only be tried after the case for the prosecution had been tested, was completely abandoned.[11] Many judges had considerable misgivings. For example, the Supreme Court in 1965 dismissed a case in which the government had considerable interest, the Commissioner of Police *versus* Akowuah. The latter was a District Commissioner who was accused of obtaining £200 from a person who he had threatened to arrest and detain under the Preventive Detention Act. The Supreme Court upheld his appeal against prosecution on the technical ground that the appropriate words 'with intent to defraud' or some other words expressing intent did not appear in the particulars of the charge which he had to meet. The judges who made this decision were attacked openly in a special issue of the University of Ghana Law Journal by one of their own colleagues and by the Director of Public Prosecutions himself. The latter interpreted the Court's decision as a direct challenge to the supremacy of Parliament.

One of the main reasons why legal reform has not been satisfactorily tackled by most of the new regimes, is the shortage of skilled manpower in the necessary drafting work. Ghana in fact had much more experience in this field than many other countries. But an important consequence of this lack of adjustment is that many states develop a new system of arbitrary rule in parallel with the traditional system devised by the colonial power. The law made by the colonial authorities was often arbitrary enough. For example, the steps taken against the Bantu ministers in Uganda were authorized through colonial ordinances. Many African Presidents have had recourse to the powers of deportation designed by the colonialists.

The transformation of the colonial security system therefore, is unlikely to be formally completed with a complete new set of procedures. There is a strong temptation to rely on established machinery, and merely to adapt the weapons of the colonial authorities for use against political opponents. Without a radical revolution, the police and the new army tend to continue to play the different roles originally designed in the colonial allocation of powers. Indeed, as will be shown later, the new regimes sometimes deliberately exaggerated this difference of role in order to encourage rivalries between the two organizations.

[11] See regulation 8 in L.I. 370/64 *Special Criminal (Amendment) Regulations*, under the *Criminal Procedure Amendment Act* (Act 238) 1964.

STRATEGY AND DEFENCE

The first feature of political competition which has been identified, the organization of political supporters into clientage or patronage groupings, affects the redefinition of military policy in both the major fields. The supply of arms and other materials from metropolitan sources can be as important in effecting the pattern of alignments in political coalitions as the efficient design of military units. An opportunity to share in the privileges of the armed forces is a form of political reward.

In one sense, the colonial authorities encouraged this attitude, because they had no difficulty in securing recruits while the security forces were regarded as organizations giving privileges as much as obligations to work. This attitude applied to the army even more strongly than to the police.

One of the first facts which any new regime had to face was the ethnic composition of its security forces. The colonial basis of recruitment tended to be regional, particularly in anglophone colonies. For example, the authorities in Nyasaland recruited largely from the Yao in the south; those in Uganda from Nilotics in the north. The KAR, serving in Kenya, were heavily dominated by Wakamba. The Fifth Battalion for example, had worked out a tribal quota which was to be used on recruiting safaris. A third of the recruits were to be Kamba, and another third Kalenjin. Another common feature in colonial policy was the predilection of those in charge of recruiting for the less educated. This meant, as in Ghana and Nigeria, that large numbers of the ordinary soldiers came from those parts of the country in the north, which had a very poorly developed educational system.

The first mark of change, therefore, made by many new regimes, was to broaden the base of recruitment. President Kenyatta in Kenya laid it down that the Kenya army should be composed as near as possible of men drawn from all tribes in the same proportion as they existed within the boundaries of the country. His expatriate advisers attempted to apply this policy as strictly as possible, but sometimes found it extremely difficult to find candidates for training on this basis. In fact the accidents of the educational pattern in Kenya meant that the President's own tribe, the Kikuyu, because they had been well supplied with a system of schools, could always present a high proportion of officer material to the selection boards. In many colonies, secondary schoolboys had not been encouraged to enlist in the army until some time in the mid-1950s, when the colonial authorities were planning a more rapid Africanization of the officer cadre.

What was the effect of the new system of political competition on redefinition of security policy? An important consequence of African access to power was the exposure of the army to proposals for expansion which were not related to any obvious military objective. Armies and police forces themselves were vulnerable to outside interference. Warring factions could seek support for their opposing causes within the ranks of the army. Unless elaborate precautions were taken, any leader who wished to further his cause might well look for support among soldiers and policemen especially if they contained members of his own tribe or region.

Ironically, the new regimes would have been better placed if they were protected by mercenary forces alone. Those who serve for money rather than out of any sense of obligation were less likely to change their allegiance. If expatriate officers could satisfactorily insulate the army in which they served from local politics, then such a body naturally took on the role of a mercenary force. Such a policy carried its own risks. A mutiny in such conditions could not be confined to questions of pay or conditions, but became automatically an attack on the regime.

Can one build a new nation by making obligatory a system of national service for the existing organizations? Or must new organizations be designed for the purpose? It might be argued that in some cases a national service army would be a direct threat to the regime. King Hussein, for example, could not really expand the Arab Legion to include a representative quota from the West Bank of the Jordan. The states of tropical Africa present two great contrasts. The first is between those who have a national service system and those who depend upon voluntary recruits. The second is between those who base their organizations primarily on colonial models, and those who have developed other models, such as people's militias, or brigades of vigilantes. In true accord with the republican tradition of France, most of the French-speaking states adopted a law for compulsory national service. But in practice, as will be explained in the next chapter, it largely provided means of extending the basis of recruitment, so that those who have shown themselves to be proficient at arms might be retained as regulars after they have finished their period of compulsory service. Except for Tanzania, the anglophone countries have retained a system of voluntary recruitment. The Tanzanian system is perhaps the most important experiment of all. President Nyerere inaugurated it in the aftermath of the mutiny which took place in January 1964. He has been helped primarily by the Canadian army and an Israeli training team in the National Service. Those regimes which have introduced people's militias have been associated with aid from the Communist bloc. Cuba has played an important part in training the militia in Congo (Brazzaville).

Major shifts in any regime's position in international affairs are important in defining the reasons for transforming the role played by colonial-type security forces. No other regime, except that of President Nkrumah in Ghana, has attempted to argue that strong national armies should be built up in order to create a Pan-African force. Nkrumah was annoyed when one of his own officers, Nathan Aferi, in a report to the Organization of African Unity (OAU) made in 1965, declined to endorse armed moves against Rhodesia on a Pan-African scale. What is the major reason for transforming a colonial army? By far the most important motive in the eyes of the majority of regimes is to build a stronger basis for their own power. A consideration of new external security threats is usually considered subordinate to this. Few countries are obliged to prepare for the serious threat of war, unless that war is a possible civil war within their own political community.

The dominant motive therefore encourages the ambitions of soldiers. They do not in fact remain passive while governments plan to transform what they might do. Indeed they expect some share in the fruits of power. Furthermore, they know very well that they can enforce their will by arms. All regimes fear a mutiny about pay and conditions. Not only may different civilian groups be competing for the support of groups inside the military, but also soldiers themselves may be looking for important and sensitive points where they can exercise a little leverage.

Every head of state therefore sees his own minister of defence as a possible source of subversion. The minister responsible for internal security has the greatest opportunity to build up his own personal following inside the security forces. The element of clientage or patronage may enter into his negotiations with the men in his charge. In certain circumstances, the army may begin itself to take on the cover of an intriguing group, which is looking for the best bargain. Amin, when as deputy commander he led a party of the Uganda Army to aid the Congolese rebels in

January 1965, had the support of an 'inner ring' of ministers and the faction in the army, without comitting the state to open war. The established procedures for promotion and for maintaining discipline are transformed if this degree of politicization comes about.

In any intrigue, support from the army may look like a short cut to power. In what circumstances do security forces themselves become the focus for political competition? The structure of police forces makes it more difficult to use them in any attempt at subversion. The army is usually more heavily concentrated in a given number of barracks, and can usually be mobilized swiftly to occupy the most strategic points in the capital. The only regime to be successfully overthrown by dissidents from its own police force was that of the Arab ZNP Government in Zanzibar. The latter made the revolution of January 1964 possible by failing to transform efficiently and swiftly the colonial police force which it had inherited. The colonial authorities maintained no army in Zanzibar, but a police force, largely recruited from mainland Africa. The policemen, as mainlanders, were naturally sympathetic with the aspirations of the chief opponents of the ZNP Government, the Afro–Shirazi Party. The new regime saw this danger to their strength, and began to dismiss the policemen and send them home, replacing them with their own supporters. But they failed to do this effectively. The revolutionaries in Zanzibar under John Okello were able to recruit supporters from policemen who had been dismissed but who had remained on the Island. They also gained from their new recruits detailed knowledge of the internal structure of the key police stations, and of the armouries kept there.[12]

When armies participate in political in-fighting, their actions usually reflect the different bases of the regimes with which they are involved. Although they have been treated as strictly comparable events, the difference between the three East African mutinies in January 1964 are in some ways more important than the similarities. There seems to have been a chain reaction among the soldiers in the KAR as a result of the Zanzibar revolution. Those looking for evidence of a plot saw it in the radical sympathies of three of the ministers involved. Kambona in Tanganyika, Onama in Uganda, and Odinga in Kenya. In fact the initiative seems to have come from the rank and file. An important difference is that those in Tanganyika and Uganda had been

[12] John Okello, *Revolution in Zanzibar* (Nairobi: East African Publishing House, 1967), pp. 18–19.

systematically exploited by politicians for more than a year, whereas the recent independence in Kenya had given few opportunities for such action. The British officers present proved an easy scapegoat. When there were threats of a mutiny the soldiers in Tanganyika and Kenya were particularly annoyed by what seemed to be the moves to protect British life and property. For example, the British staff officers, who arrived at the Eleventh Battalion (KAR) barracks in Kenya to brief the Commanding Officer on preparations to suppress the mutiny, did not act discreetly, but arrived in uniform and with a staff car. The men lost faith in British officers, as protectors of their interests. By the time Colonel Mans arrived in October 1963 to command the Tanganyika Rifles, he and his RSM were the only British with sufficient war-time KAR experience to speak fluent Swahili. The British lost face and therefore the power to command. Of the major differences, the Tanganyikan mutiny looks the only one in which there might have been a deliberate plan worked out by those outside the army. The minister concerned, Oscar Kambona, played, to say the least, a rather ambivalent role. British officers thought that he was directly involved in subverting the army against them. He had certainly subjected them to some rather pointed snubs. It looks as if African officers and N.C.O.s in Tanganyika were not directly involved. Captain Nyirenda was in fact regarded by the minister almost as a personal opponent. All N.C.O.s seem to have been directly responsible for events in Uganda and Kenya. The British presence in Uganda was a handicap to the plans which were already being made by Obote and Onama for strengthening their regime through the army. The foolish behaviour of some expatriates at a Christmas party on Tank Hill in 1963 strengthened their hand. The split between Nilotics and Bantu in the Uganda army was already apparent. Onama knew that the army was the Nilotics' chief defence. The split between Luo and Kikuyu in Kenyan politics did not appear in the army because neither tribe was strongly represented in military circles, although a considerable number of Luo served in certain technical sections, such as the Signals. This fact alone is one of the chief reasons for the British staying on to guide the Kenyan army to further development. When President Obote and Nyerere rejected British aid, the Kenyans were pleased to accept it. The composition of an army can therefore be crucial in determining the part it might play in the creation of a new regime. The acute rivalries of political groupings in Uganda and Nigeria for example, quickly penetrated into the military apparatus. In Uganda the ruling group was able to take advantage of Nilotic predominance in the Army to rally support against those who were trying to use other minority groups as a basis of revolution. In Nigeria, the minority Ibo group inside the army struck first, and thus destroyed the existing regime and endangered the whole coherence of the army itself.

Various comparisons have been made between these two cases. Traditional rulers were involved in each, and the chief issue was the preservation of the traditional forms of government within a federal system. The main contrast was between the nature of the two regimes. The Ugandan government was strongly opposed to the preservation inside Uganda of the Kingdom of Buganda with a special set of privileges. The Nigerian government, on the other hand, was deliberately composed in such a way that representatives from the northern region should predominate. The plots in these two countries were therefore from opposite ends of the scale. The Ibo officers who planned the assassinations of northern ministers, and the destruction of the federal government, appear to have wished to abolish the traditional pattern of chiefly rule. The Bantu ministers in Uganda who plotted to overthrow President Obote were prepared to strike in order that the Bantu kingdoms might be preserved within the federal structure. The Kabaka of Buganda appears to have placed great trust in the Teso elements of the Uganda army, as well as in those Bantu officers who disliked the regime. Two of the accused ministers, Ibingira and Magezi, had kinsmen in the officer corps, R. Katabarwa and D. G. Ndahura. Some interpretations of the first Nigerian *coup* in January 1966 have suggested that the principal political leader in the north, the Sardauna of Sokoto, had been planning to use the army against dissident elements in the western region in order to establish his power. There is little evidence to support this interpretation, but it is important that it has been believed. Both these countries demonstrate how readily people believed that warring factions would carry on their contest right inside the army itself.

The fight to establish support inside the Uganda army began soon after independence. The British commanding officer found a minister intriguing among the soldiers in the barracks within a month of the regime taking power. Within six weeks of independence, one of the ministers, Kirya, who was later imprisoned for his part in the plot, had sent some of his proteges for military training in Israel, without informing or consulting British officers, who were still nominally in command of the army. The very serious external security problems facing Uganda on its borders, due both to refugees from Ruanda, the Congo and the Sudan, as well as secessionist movements in Toro, obliged the government to expand its armed forces rapidly. The original independence government was a coalition between natural opposites, the Uganda People's Congress (UPC), largely dominated by northern elements, and Kabaka Yekka, the monarchist party of Buganda. While this coalition lasted, it was possible to encourage a policy of broadening the base for recruitment to the army, so that Bantu, particularly Baganda, could be included. But after the collapse of the coalition in September 1964, and particularly after the UPC gained an overall majority in the House, it became increasingly obvious that the Nilotic group within the UPC were using the army as a base for their power.[13] Ministers were even able to joke about the Baganda who had run away when they debated the creation of the Third Battalion in the Autumn of 1964.[14] After the Uganda army's operations in the Congo, to aid the rebellion based on Stanleyville, which had been led by the Deputy Army Commander, Colonel Amin, the army began to polarize between the predominant group of Nilotics under Amin, who came himself from West Nile, and the Teso Bantu group, led by the Army Commander, Brigadier Opolot. By the summer of 1965, when Kabaka Yekka decided to attack the UPC from inside by organizing its members in a massive walk over to the Buganda branch of the UPC it seemed difficult to avoid armed conflict. Many people thought that President Obote would be overthrown, and it is alleged that a first attempt was made on his life in October 1965.

In Nigeria, the contest for military support was not played out so openly. General Whistler as Colonel Commandant had expressed fears about the tension already growing between northerners and southerners in the army, when he visited it in 1961.[15] These divisions showed themselves as divisions between officers and men. The troops were largely northern, and the officers were predominantly southern, particularly in the technical sections of the army. Ghanaian officers visiting Nigeria at the same period reported that life in the mess had been strongly affected by tribal divisions, in such things as the use of the vernacular instead of

[13] Mutesa, Kabaka of Buganda, *Desecration of My Kingdom* (London: Nelson, 1967), p. 79.
[14] *Uganda National Assembly Debates*, Vol. 35, p. 3199.
[15] '*Bolo*' Whistler, *op. cit.*, pp. 230–1.

English, and social and sporting groupings. But the British officers in charge manfully tried to overcome these divergencies. It is more difficult to prove that politicians thought of strengthening their position by the army, but it is clear that such a method of resolving political differences was in the minds of those who discussed with President Azikiwe in the reconstruction of the government after the federal elections of 1964. The presence of a British General, Welby-Everard, did something to inhibit the possible employment of the army for political ends.

The most important consequence of political factions entering into army life was the threat which they constituted to discipline. While British officers were present, normal colonial procedures were pursued, but General Ironsi, for example, when he succeeded Welby-Everard, in 1965, found that tribal considerations entered into court-martial procedure. When any officer was accused of mis-using ministry funds for his own purposes, he could only be tried after it had been possible to find men from other tribes to stand with him.

Even where the composition of security forces was not so vulnerable to political infiltration, the rivalries of civilian groups could still find expression in a division between existing military units. It was common practice for individual politicians to find that they were better placed in regard to one kind of security force than to another. David Dacko, the President of the Central African Republic, deliberately cultivated the gendarmerie as a means of counteracting the influence of his kinsman, Colonel Bokassa, the Commander of the Army. Provincial political ambition in the Congo has always found support in the provincial gendarmerie. One of General Mobutu's first actions after taking power in 1965 was to bring the police under firm control. Even where military units did not provide a basis of opposition to the regime, those in power sometimes thought it wise to deliberately encourage professional rivalries. Nkrumah in 1964 made a point of humiliating the army by giving Ferret scout-cars to the police. Any moves which gave the police forces greater military firepower, in the form of special units or riot squads, could be interpreted as a means of limiting the army's freedom of movement.

The political importance of established units and security forces is that few leaders are strong enough to abolish them. They represent systems of patronage because they are an important part of a state's power to create jobs. Even Congo (Brazzaville) did not dare to abolish the existing army when the decision was taken to establish a people's militia trained by the Cubans. The army was weakened by losing its French training team, but it was not totally destroyed. A post in the security forces carries considerable political weight, and offers important opportunities to the holder's family. Few officers were asked to resign for technical incompetence; those who were dismissed or removed have usually been involved in political activities which are unacceptable to the regime. Only where expatriate officers are still in command, as in Kenya, Malawi, or Sierra Leone before 1965 have officers been relieved of their commissions on personal grounds which have no connection with politics.

The design of new military units is therefore greatly affected by a new regime's interpretation of its position. What kind of units can a new state afford? Most of the leaders of new states have set in motion plans for the development of mobile units, or security companies. One of the motives of President Kenyatta in sending a company to Britain for parachute training in April 1965 was a display of his power against his political opponents. Parachute companies have become almost an essential prestige symbol. They usually command first priority after the formation of the normal support units with each battalion, such as, transport, signals, and engineering. Few African armies have developed any heavy armour. The emphasis has been on making the best trained infantry units and transport. Several francophone states have followed the French example of creating Republican Security Companies. The anglophone equivalents are special units inside the police force.

Planning a completely new system of security for a new state may face simple problems of finance as well as concrete political difficulties. For example, the five-year plan in Sierre Leone, devised by Brigadier Blackie in 1960, rested on the argument that the interests of the country would best be served if a third battalion was formed, and if that battalion was dispersed throughout the country as the basis of a training system for a territorial reserve. This idea has never been implemented, largely because of its cost. The economic considerations were less important if solid political advantages could be gained from an expansion. Albert Margai as Prime Minister of Sierra Leone relied largely on his contacts with the army commander, Colonel David Lansana,[16] and not on building up a party inside the army. Kenyatta

---

[16] Not to be confused with Diane Lansana, the commander in Guinea. The fact that both speak the same language strengthened the ties between their respective heads of state.

in Kenya, for example, saw that he could use the army and the national youth service as a means of making some contribution to the great and growing problem of unemployment in the towns. Some of the dissatisfaction felt by secondary school leavers could be met by the jobs created in a security system.

The redefinition of security policy has therefore been heavily influenced by the political demands of the moment. In determining both the origin of military supplies and in the design of military units new governments have been strongly influenced by the political pay-offs which they envisaged. Sometimes, as will be explained in the next chapter, decisions about overseas aid and military assistance from overseas countries were taken on the basis of profit to individual ministers. Israel has been particularly skilful at exploiting this African weakness. It is hard to explain some of the movements of policy except in terms of personal assessments of advantage.

THE RANGE OF CHOICE

The choices each new regime could make in terms of military supply, or the design of security units, were usually made in terms of the political calculations of the moment. There were considerable differences between the methods pursued in anglophone states and in francophone states. The former had a much greater range of choice because they received from the colonial authorities security forces which were already operational within the recognized boundaries of the state. The latter on the other hand, depended on French assistance in the reconstruction of French units, which had been liable to service anywhere within the French community. Except in Guinea and Mali, which have been described above, each francophone state began life in a much more dependent posture than its equivalent anglophone.

Colonial habits and methods of work were just as difficult to supersede as their uniforms and their matériel. African soldiers and policemen found that their role in the new community still depended a great deal on colonial precedents, and upon the accidents of colonial design. There was less confusion in the mind of each individual if the new regime accepted fully the continuance of links with the metropolitan power. Sir Milton Margai, as the first Prime Minister of Sierra Leone, left the management of his army entirely to its British Commander, and declined to call regular meetings of the Defence Council, as the Governor had done in colonial days. He trusted the British, and had really no desire for fundamental change. Dr Banda, the President of Malawi, has made it clear to his officers and men that he intends to pursue a policy of retaining expatriate officers for a long time to come. His security forces are based on the assumption that Africanization will come only slowly. The individual soldier or policeman finds it easier to avoid being confused about his position if the new regime and its security forces share a common culture. In Uganda or in Chad the men in the security forces find it easy to identify their new masters. The greatest confusion occurs where the colonial security system relies upon men who are very unsympathetic to the new nationalist Government.

Extensive uncertainty among the people is much more widespread than confusion among the office-holders. Those brought into the political community of the state by the accidents of colonial boundaries can only be brought into a common political culture through either a common experience, or some clearly radical leadership. In looking for a way to set limits on the system of competition for the very limited resources which a new state could distribute, many people naturally fall back on the traditional units and the traditional methods of political communication which existed before the colonial authorities were established.

The remarkable success of Somalia is a standing reminder of the handicaps under which other states laboured. One of the difficulties faced by Somalis in framing their foreign policy is that they do not realize how exceptional their experience has been. The Somalis did not need to learn nationalism from the first independent regime. The whole basis of the Somali claim to independence was to extend the boundaries of the new state beyond those which the colonial authorities have recognized, in order to bring within the new Somalia all those Somalis living in French Somaliland, Ethiopia, and Kenya. Furthermore, the appeal of Somali irredentism is based on the cultural unity of Islam. The extraordinary achievement of Somalia is that it was able within four years of independence to integrate the two separate administrations which formed the basis of the colonial states, British Somaliland Protectorate and Italian Somaliland, and also to unite the security forces of both these colonies into a new army and a new police force. All this was done in spite of the difficulties of having two languages, English and Italian, and two different sets of legal rules, from two separate colonial powers, Britain and Italy.

By the time of the 1964 elections, it was clear all Somali politicians accepted certain unwritten principles. All parties and governments were based upon coalitions of the traditional clans in Somali society. It was accepted that all governments should be multiclan coalitions, and the two chief officers of state, President and Prime Minister, should not be held by members of the same clan. The nature of shifting alliances between the clans prevented the new state from splitting between north and south, that is between the old British sector and the old Italian sector. The Darod clan was the largest and the most widely scattered. Its network of connections had always provided links between the two former colonies. But this clan alone could not control the whole country, and it was in the interests of the others that strife among the Darods be encouraged. Between elections the dissidents of all clans are able to reconstruct the political parties. It is significant that Somalia has never developed a 'Father of the Nation' kind of figure, such as Jomo Kenyatta in neighbouring Kenya. Elections have effected changes of government, and no single person has remained in power. All acknowledge the importance of clan alliances, and of the patronage which the leaders of each clan secure for their supporters. Somalia shares one feature with other African states, the desire to make sure that national politics reflect directly local rivalries. But it is able to cultivate this direct link between local and national affairs without endangering the whole state apparatus. During the period of internal self-government in Italian Somaliland before independence, the Somali Youth League chose as its first Prime Minister Abdirahid Ali Shirmarke, largely because he had a certain edge over other candidates in the Darod faction through his possession of a degree in political science. This principle of choice was an augury of future style.

After independence the amalgamation of the two colonial security forces into a new national police and army was, like the government, on a multiclan basis. The British Somaliland police and the Italian gendarmerie, was commanded by General Daud, who came from the Hawiye clan, one of the Darod's traditional rivals. Although the former gendarmerie had contained a large proportion of Darod, the newly constructed security forces reflected the clan structure of the nation fairly closely. When British military support for the army ceased in 1963 after the break in diplomatic relations, the Russians gave it massive aid. The United States, which was already the major support to the army's traditional enemy, Ethiopia, could hardly join in this assistance. But the Somalis accepted American support for an extended police force and gendarmerie. Such was Somali confidence in the workability of their system that they knew that the principle of clan balance would work against any attempt to set the army against the police or vice versa.

The Somali experience demonstrates that one cannot measure political instability by changes of government, but by the absence of an agreed set of rules. Nor is the amount of personal violence an appropriate index. Murder is common in Somalia; blood feuds are an accepted way of settling disputes between clans; the gun is a symbol of virility for every young man. The colonial authorities in British Somaliland made no serious attempt to destroy the predominance of clan loyalties. The local district police force, the Illalos, were recruited from local clans. It was an excellent testimony to the principle of clan balance, even in colonial days, that when the Illalos were called upon to stop an inter-clan fight, the police restored order by dividing into their own clan groups, each of which fired upon the opponents of its own kin. Police coherence was retained because nobody was called upon to oppose his own family.

What other new states can show such a highly developed basis for political action as that of Somalia? The Sudan and Ethiopia have a sufficiently distinctive political culture to enable them to find a satisfactory role for their security forces. Both, especially the latter, are vulnerable to a military revolution which claims to reconstruct the social system. But neither has an army which is likely to behave as an autonomous organization. A breakdown in the structure of command is unlikely in countries which have such a high degree of homogeneity, and where the security forces are closely integrated into the political system. Somalia, the Sudan, and Ethiopia naturally stand in contrast to the new states of tropical Africa. How closely can the latter approach to the Somali system of stability? The possession of a dominant group culture, particularly if it is associated with traditional systems of authority, or traditional pre-colonial patterns of rule, is a tremendous advantage in the growth of a new political system.

Many commentators have argued that one of the strengths behind the socialist regimes of Guinea and Mali is that the Fouta Djallon district of Guinea and the Niger River Basin part of Mali were the centres of the pre-colonial empires. The new rulers can appeal to political values of considerable antiquity. Similarly, the politics of Senegal reflect the supremacy of the Wolof tribe.

Wolof methods of organizing political support have been built into the ruling party, the UPS by President Senghor.

For many new states the features of the Somali system which bring stability are in fact those which bring them nearest to collapse. The history of the Congo seems much more relevant to the new regimes than that of Somalia. That is why so few Africans take an interest in the latter. If the traditional cleavages of local politics are allowed to dominate at the national level, there is a constant danger of excessive competition which will exhaust all the parties concerned. If outside aid from rival super-powers, such as Russia and the United States, is brought in behind warring factions, then no indigenous political system can grow. Features which unite the nation where there is a common culture, bring chaos and confusion where there is not.

General Mobutu, since he seized power in the Congo in November 1965, has concentrated his attention on precisely these two points of weakness. First, he has reconstructed the whole provincial system of government. In April 1966 he reduced the number of Congolese provinces from 21 to 12, and the following December, from 12 to 8. The election of new provincial governors, which was carried out by the provincial assemblies, gave him an opportunity to destroy the power base of a large number of his opponents. He regards his new system as unitary, but decentralized. Although it can be partly seen as part of his determination to rally former Lumumbist sentiment, his decision to nationalize the Belgian mining company, *Union Minière*, was aimed at destroying the permanent threat to secession which that company could finance in Katanga. After lengthy negotiations, Mobotu had to come to terms with Belgian interests, in order to get Congolese copper refined and sold on the world market. But he had made an important psychological victory. A reminder of the continuous danger of provincial revolt lay in the activities of the Katangese gendarmerie and their allied European mercenaries. Mobutu announced that the Mulelist revolt had been brought under control in April 1966, only to find himself facing both a plot against his government and a new mutiny of the Katangese gendarmerie a few months later. It is perhaps a tribute to the extent of his control that the mutiny of mercenaries which began in July 1967, and was associated in the minds of the government with a plot to restore Tshombe to the Congo, should have been linked to a mercenary army in Angola, and not to part of the provincial structure of the Republic.

Secondly, Mobutu reconstructed the Congolese army with a planned diversification of military aid. The proposals which he had made in the spring of 1963 to build up an army of 25,000 men led to a series of bilateral agreements which were to be put into force before the United Nations withdrew its forces in June 1964. Belgium agreed to plan the organization of the army, and to provide training centres; Israel undertook the training of parachutists; Canada, to provide aid for the Navy; Italy to train the air force; and the United States to supply a wide range of material to all forces. This deliberate division of responsibilities looked like a new version of the Ethiopian model. The aid given to the air force caused the greatest diplomatic difficulties, because of its operational importance in the campaign against the mutineers. The United Nations had previously supplied the pilots for military transport planes. Italy had difficulty in maintaining its air-force mission, and the campaign against the rebels depended to a considerable extent upon an air-force team from Belgium, and on American aid. Although the Chinese continued to abuse his regime as an American puppet, Mobutu was able to demonstrate that military aid from different sources did not necessarily introduce insurmountable political rivalries. Somalia and the Congo began from opposite ends of the scale in the construction of the state apparatus. The Somalis learnt the limits of political action from the conventions of traditional clan rivalries. The Congolese were presented with new rules of behaviour by a military government. The majority of states formed by the peaceful transfer of power fell closer to the Congolese model, if not to Congolese solutions.

In the absence of civil order, a military organization finds it easier to retain a sense of identity and to avoid the risks of internal collapse if the competition for power explodes into open civil war. But in the majority of cases in tropical Africa so far political conflict has been expressed in plots and counter-plots, repression and sporadic rebellion, but not in outright warfare. The established authorities of the state have had some success in limiting the use of violence. Yet they have little range of choice when the political community is not sufficiently aware of its common interests to impose restraints on its members.

Chapter Four

THE MILITARY IN THE POLITICAL COMMUNITY

I T is not easy to distinguish between military and social values. The army can prevent a sudden collapse of government, but it is by no means clear that it can contribute to the growth of civil order. How far can soldiers and policemen create and diffuse new values in society? How far can they in fact help to remove some of the basic obstacles in the path of economic development?

Maintaining coherence and efficiency inside the security forces became increasingly difficult after independence, because the values generated within the context of opportunity which it created were not those inculcated by the organizations inherited from the colonial power. The type of organization on a clan or village basis, which could be developed by indigenous concepts of security and self-defence, was not appropriate for international recognition as part of the state aparatus. The new states were obliged to arm themselves with instruments of coercion which could be used against violent expressions of feeling within the political community. But the latter was now in a position from which to subvert them. The personal ties which held soldiers and policemen to their families and friends acquired a new significance.

A basic feature of political competition was that frustration frequently brought a recourse to violence. Particularly among those who had migrated to the towns, the key to personal success lay in education. Society was conceived in fairly open terms, but access to positions of power or profit within the state apparatus were seen to depend on educational qualifications. Societies were rocked by tensions generated in the fight to succeed the white man. Violence and destruction became means for relieving personal feelings. All those who observed the elections in the western region of Nigeria in October 1965 have described the banditry which followed in terms of popular disgust for the accepted procedures and institutions of the state. Instead of channelling their energies into a political reform movement, the young men robbed the rich and destroyed property with no clear end in view. African societies move perilously close to this chaotic condition. Many people see their political salvation, not in terms of law, or of accepted procedures of public business, but in alliances with influential people, or in expressions of supernatural power. When opponents are accused of witchcraft or officials of corruption, criticism is rarely made in institutional terms, but in terms of personal grievance. It is difficult to prepare for such outbreaks of violence, and to insulate security forces from the environment which breeds them.

People living in the new states find natural outlets for their feelings in movements of a more communal basis. Direct experience of military organization usually belongs to this level. Bourgoignie, while he was working for the Youth Commission in Bukavu, before Congolese independence, received a telegram from an officially sponsored youth club announcing that it had transformed itself into a club of bandits. The young people disappeared into the bush in search of any politicians who might pass through the region.[1] After the revolution in Brazzaville in 1963, Pierre Erny thought that the young people who constituted the *Brigades de Vigilance* were primarily interested in the magical qualities given to them by the exercise of power over the rest of the population. They enjoyed stopping cars and searching them. Similar expressions of morale can be found in the religious sects which seemed to be associated with societies undergoing this degree of strain. Welbourn and Ogot have described the impact of these movements on East Africa.[2] The sect which acquired an international notoriety was the Lumpa Church under Alice Lenshina, whose activities were only suppressed after an extensive military operation in Zambia during 1964 and 1965.

Such expressions of popular sentiment are hardly in accord with the organization and training given to security forces on the colonial model. The latter are better attuned to maintaining the state apparatus on lines which would meet with the approval of the outside powers which created it. The transfer of power was a process which resulted from the clash between nationalist aspirations inside each territory and the assessment made by the colonial authorities of their position in international affairs. Soldiers and policemen were caught in the cross-fire between two interpretations of legitimate authority.

[1] G-E Bourgoignie, *Jeune Afrique Mobilisable* (Brussels: Editions Universitaires, 1964), p. 105 n.
[2] F. B. Welbourn and B. A. Ogot, *A Place to feel at Home* (London: Oxford University Press, 1966).

It is difficult to define political order in terms which do not seem either too western or too legalistic. Lucian Pye has argued that in the Burmese political system people turn to participation in politics in order to escape from the more morbid aspects of their Buddhist religion. He thinks that the Burmese prefer uncertainty or unpredictable change in their political system because Buddhist doctrines of determinism are distasteful.[3] Africa contains far too many religions and cultures for such an argument to be an acceptable interpretation of African conditions. But there appears to be a preference for concepts of order which do not appear to depend entirely upon a political élite. The definition of a legal system used by Professor Hart seems to imply that the development of secondary rules, the rules which govern how primary rules are to be employed, is the work of those who are privileged to run the state apparatus. Such definitions are difficult to use in the African context, primarily because all privileges seem to stem from government, and access to privilege is the chief bone of political contention. Are soldiers and policemen only familiar with definitions which originate from the colonial environment? Unless the army intervenes in politics, soldiers seem to make little contribution to the evolution of political ideas inside their own country. But once they are in a position of power, their relationships with the civilian élite are crucial to future planning. The frustrations felt by soldiers are on a par with those of civilians. What values do military regimes bring to the system? The basis of order seems to be the presence of institutions and procedures in which the political community expresses sufficient faith, so that there are recognized means of reducing tension.

The state of military law in Africa is not a good augury for the future of military inventiveness in constructing new procedures and institutions. Most of the francophone armies still cling to the tradition of French military law. The British officer who returned to the Sudan in 1963 to help with the foundation of the Staff College found that the Sudanese army was still using British military manuals and instructions issued more than ten years previously. It was perhaps a tribute to the strength of local custom in the Sudan that the country managed for a long time with only an interim constitution. Most of the states of tropical Africa have completely transformed the constitutions which were laid down by the departing colonial powers. But few have had

[3] L. W. Pye, *Politics, Personality and Nation Building* (New Haven: Yale University Press, 1962), pp. 52–55.

real experience of redrafting military law. It is necessary to get a clear definition of the role of the army, before making new rules of discipline. The retention of colonial procedures makes it difficult to discover what informal rules have developed. Only the Tanzanaian People's Defence Forces and the Ghana Armed Forces, both with the aid of Canadian legal draftsmen, have arrived at an acceptable set of formulae for the new political situation.

What is the position of the security forces in the development of new political procedures and institutions? The political conditions themselves almost preclude any rigorous analyses of this question. The statistics available are very uneven, and there are a large number of variables which have to be investigated. An outside observer faces the added difficulty of traditional attitudes to race and social position. In the detection of crime and the application of the rules of prosecution, the Ghanaian police, for example, continue to treat white men differently from their own people. African army officers are so accustomed to being judged by expatriate visitors in terms of their affiliations with the West or with the East, that all conversations between the black and the white may be less than frank. Military advisers know that they can exploit African feelings of inferiority in technological matters. But apart from these difficulties, the main features of the situation are strikingly obvious.

LIMITED RESOURCES

The basic weakness of any regime in tropical Africa is that the prizes available in the public sector are not infinitely expandable. Conditions of political competition are such that plans for the increase of the national income are the least likely to arouse interest. It seems much more important that those in power should be able to satisfy their own sense of self-importance, and to secure jobs for themselves and their friends. The resources of the state are limited by the accidents of geography and by the economic system established under colonial authority; the competition to exploit them is only limited by the conventions of the developing political system.

A brutal fact about the allocation of state resources is that the army seems to be in the best position to exploit whatever is available. It has been calculated that the Congolese army received one-sixth of the state's revenue in the first fifty-six months after independence, 25 billion out of 150 billion Congolese francs. But even this proportion is not considered exceptionally high. For example, in the provisions of the revenue budgets for 1967–68 in francophone Africa, 8 out of 15 states had provided the army with between 15 per cent and 25 per cent of their resources. Those at the top of the scale, Mali, Guinea, Chad, and Cameroun, were therefore prepared to devote up to a quarter of their budgets for military purposes.

The army's strength in taking such a high proportion of state revenue would perhaps not be so significant if the budgets were not frequently running up large deficits. Public finances are subject to an almost structural weakness. They are subject to more demands than the revenues or financial devices can bear. The most notorious example of an almost uncontrollable deficit is that of Dahomey. Even before independence, in 1959, the budget deficit was already running at 240 million CFA francs (£0·35 million). By 1961 this figure had risen to 1,165 million (£1·7 million) and by the time of the fourth *coup d'état* in 1967, it had only been reduced to 900 million CFA francs (£1·32 million). Deficit financing in the Franc Zone is a more difficult method of budgetary management to establish than in anglophone countries, because each country does not have an independent state bank. Some anglophone countries have had similar problems. For example, Sierra Leone, whose pattern of trade with Britain makes it very similar to the francophone ties with France, accepted the conditions laid down by the IMF (International Monetary Fund) in an agreement designed to tackle the principal budgetary and balance of payments problems. Before granting the loan which came into force in November 1966, the Fund insisted that the budget deficit for the following year should be reduced from 19·3 to 7·2 million Leone (£9·65 to £3·6 million).

In the francophone states, there have been such important budgetary difficulties that it has become almost a necessary condition for economic health, and for continued French support, that the budgets should be managed under a system devised by French business consultants, *Société Internationale d'Etudes de Recherches et d'Organization* (SINORG). At the beginning of 1966, France insisted that Dahomey should employ this firm before it would agree to continue giving support to the Dahomean budget. The firm had already proved its efficiency in the management of the budgets of three of the most prosperous states, Ivory Coast, Senegal, and Gabon. At the same time a political crisis developed in the Cameroun, because the President wished to employ this firm, and was opposed by the Minister of Finance himself, Victor Kanga. The latter's opposition to any reorganization of the public accounts marked the first move in a personal contest with the President. He was demoted in the Cabinet in July 1966, and arrested in November on charges of subversion. The same firm manages the budgets of three other states, the Central African Republic, Chad, and Congo (Brazzaville).

The public sector in most new states became the object of political competition because its rewards carried the greatest prestige and sense of achievement. This factor is important whether or not the government is also the chief employer of wage labour. A high proportion of all government budgets goes on salaries. A bank survey of the budgets in West Africa for 1963 showed that the proportion of current expenditure used to pay public employees varied from 37 per cent in the Ivory Coast to 63 per cent in Togo.[4] But such figures do not necessarily mean that the government is responsible for the greater part of the wage employment sector in all countries. An International Labour organization survey argued that, for anglophone Africa at any rate, the percentage of wage earners in the public sector was more likely to be between 15 per cent and 20 per cent of the total.[5] Whatever the exact proportions may be, wage earners are likely to be politically more articulate in countries where they form a minority of the active population. Subsistence farming is still the basis of much African life, and wage employment often a part-time activity.

The colonial education system is partly responsible for associating prestige with employment in the public sector. Peter Lloyd, in his analysis of the Ghanaian census for 1960, has pointed out that 40,000 of the 60,000 professionals at that date were employed in the public sector. Of the 13,000 administrators, only 3,200 were self-employed, compared with 6,100 in the public and 3,700 in the private sector.[6] To anyone with the appropriate educational qualifications, the chief alternative to government was a job with the former colonial power, *la douce métropole*. Ghanaians who disliked Nkrumah's regime always found it easy to get a job with one of the international agencies, or the United Nations itself. There are more men from Dahomey

[4] 'Essai d'Analyse Économique et Fonctionelle des Budgets des États de l'Afrique de l'Ouest', *BCEAO Note d'Information*, No. 105, April 1964.

[5] K. C. Doctor and H. Gallis, 'Size and characteristics of Wage Employment in Africa', *International Labour Review*, Vol. 93 (2), February 1966.

[6] P.C. Lloyd, *Africa in Social Change* (Harmondsworth: Penguin, 1967), p. 144.

trained in medicine working in the Paris region than in Dahomey itself.

A major threat to any regime therefore is that state employees lose confidence in the value of the privileges granted by the state apparatus. The military regimes in Dahomey and Upper Volta were constructed in 1966, after major civil service discontent with the austerity budgets. The demonstrators in the streets of Ouagadougou carried placards bearing the slogan: 'We, the 0·09 per cent' a reference to the fact that President Yaméogo claimed he had received 99·01 per cent of the votes in the election which took place in the preceding October. Whatever its style of budget management, no regime can easily control the opposition of its own agents, although they might appear to be striking against themselves. Inflation devalues the profits of office; austerity budgets limit the resources available. The point of collapse in the state apparatus is easily reached, if the demands made upon its resources are too great, or if the incumbents of office object to a loss of status, and refuse to work.

In any reconstruction of the budget, the salaries of the army seem the least likely to be touched. The Ghanaian National Liberation Council gave the army a 5 per cent salary increase after the *coup*. The military regime in Upper Volta after the *coup* of 1966 decided that those soldiers who served in civilian posts should retain their military salaries, and not be transferred to the civilian wage structure where austerity cuts had been made. Largely because it feared that the army might be tempted to interfere in a delicate political situation, the government of Mali, in its austerity measures of 1966, decided not to include the army in the cuts which it was making. This military privilege was excused on the grounds that the army was fighting a war against the Touareg. Fear of the army, even when the latter is not in control, places it in a strong position.

Nowhere is the retention of 'Senior Service' expatriate salaries more obvious than in the security forces themselves. Particularly among the officer cadre, there has been a deliberate policy of comparability with metropolitan armies, the francophone states with the French, and the anglophone with the British (see Table Five). An African colonel in anglophone Africa expects to begin with a starting salary of about £2,500 without allowances.

Salary scales are an important indication of the way in which African armies look abroad for their standards. The army tries to preserve a certain international standing. One cannot easily cut military salaries without losing some face. For example, in

1967 an officer cadet from Tanzania at the Mons Officer Cadet School in England earning £24 a month might find himself alongside a Zambian cadet earning £46, almost twice as much. Because officers' salaries are deliberately kept at something near the expatriate level, there are vast differences in personal status and power between officers and men. The Lieutenant-Colonel of the battalion may be earning as much as ten or fifteen times the wage, as a starting salary, of his ordinary recruits. The equivalent differential in Britain and France is about five times the recruit's wage. These great differences were maintained in both anglophone and francophone states, although the latter usually maintain French salaries at the 1960 level, and have not increased them greatly since. Other ranks in anglophone states have received pay increases, but their wages are more comparable to African conditions of service in colonial days than to those of expatriates.

Nevertheless, the ordinary soldier and policeman belongs to some kind of élite, whatever definition is used to separate those in stable wage employment from the rest. For a seminar held in Ibadan in July 1964, Peter Lloyd defined the African élite in terms of those who had received some form of western education and could command an income of more than £250 ($700 at 1964 prices) or 150,000 CFA francs.[7] Even after allowance has been made for changes in the cost of living since that date, by this definition the average non-commissioned officer in African armies belongs to the élite. A sergeant can expect to earn something between £250 and £500 a year; senior warrant officers and regimental sergeant majors may earn up to £800 or £900. Police pay is generally a little lower than this, but not markedly so. The majority of police sergeants expect at least £300 a year, and in the inspectorate salaries vary between £400 and £800, except in Zambia where the legacy of a white inspectorate has produced a much higher salary scale (see Table Five). The wages of the security forces therefore compare very favourably with the survey carried out by the International Labour organization of work at a clerical level, for example, wholesale grocery clerks and bank tellers.[8] What is the relationship of an élite so defined

[7] P. C. Lloyd (editor), *The New Élites of Tropical Africa*, (London: Oxford University Press, 1966).

[8] The range of salaries for clerical work in the anglophone countries included in this survey (Ghana, Malawi, Nigeria, Tanzania and Uganda) is wide, e.g. bank tellers in Ghana earned £306, in Uganda £700. This survey was made in October 1966.

TABLE FIVE (a)

ANGLOPHONE
ARMY SALARIES: 1967

The annual starting salaries for each rank without allowances: in pounds
sterling at current rates of exchange before devaluation

	Kenya	Uganda	Zambia	Malawi	Nigeria	Ghana	Sierra Leone
Major-General	–	–	–	–	–	2,777	
Commander	–	2,900	–	–	–		
Brigadier	2,520	2,500	3,066	–	2,700	2,410	2,850
Colonel	2,175	2,300	2,691	2,440	2,250	2,095	2,500
Lt. Colonel	1,935	1,935	2,217	2,000	1,960	1,739	2,150
Major	1,690	1,690	1,779	1,271	1,392	1,307	1,432
Captain	1,200	1,200	1,368	954	1,164	1,014	1,128
Lieutenant	905	905	1,003	668	810	819	876
2/Lieutenant	790	790	949	615	768	734	720
Cadet	312	516	638	312	420	–	525
RSM	813	–	766	500	492	–	384
WO1	813	963	784	455	492	630	384
WO2	525	648	547	383	396	544	324
Sergeant	316	510	370	242	300	504	240
Corporal	194	–	292	161	264	390	210
Private	129	285	180	108	200	300	159

TABLE FIVE (b)

ANGLOPHONE
POLICE SALARIES

The annual starting salaries for each rank without allowances; in pounds
sterling at current rates of exchange before devaluation

	Kenya	Uganda	Zambia	Malawi	Ghana	Nigeria	Sierra Leone
Year	1966–7	1966–7	1963	1967	1967	1966–7	1967–8
Inspector General	–	3,100*	–	–	3,000	3,360	–
Deputy Inspector General	–	2,700*	–	–	–	2,940	–
Commissioner	2,800	–	3,390	–	2,500	2,820	2,500
Deputy Commissioner	2,400	–	2,990	–	2,200	2,476	2,250
Senior Assistant Commissioner	2,175	2,500*	2,790	–	–	–	–
Assistant Commissioner	1,839	–	2,590	–	1,900	2,292	2,150
Senior Superintendent	1,442	–	2,225	1,654	1,570	1,860	1,600
Superintendent	1,264	–	1,985	1,276	1,190	1,368	1,284
Assistant Superintendent	820	–	–	716	740	1,164	660
Deputy Assistant Superintendent	–	–	–	–	–	690	–
Cadet	–	–	–	–	–	–	–
Senior Chief Inspector	812	–	1,630	–	–	726	670
Inspector	682	–	1,165	509	(1)650 (2)550 (3)450	489	570
Assistant Sub Inspector	339	455	(1)915 (2)640 (3)465	414	–	381	438
Head Constable Major	–	481	–	414	–	–	–
Head Constable	–	400	–	366	–	–	–
Sergeant Major	–	–	–	–	(1)480 (2)430	–	–
Station Sergeant	–	342	–	–	–	–	–
1st Sergeant	–	–	–	284	–	–	–
2nd Sergeant	–	–	–	219	–	–	–
Sergeant	237	301	–	–	380	303	276
Corporal	209	238	–	–	330	267	225
Constable	153	192	–	115	(1)260 (2)220 (3)180	174	156

* Estimates

to the rest of the population? How far does such an élite behave as if it were a social class? The answers to these questions form the basis of the Marxist case against the power of the 'state bourgeoisie' in Africa.

The security forces were clearly a costly part of the state apparatus. The budgetary estimates in anglophone Africa for 1966 to 1967 suggest that any government wishing to maintain a single battalion of infantry might be required to pay up to £400,000 a year in salaries alone. To put such a battalion in the field, with appropriate stores, travelling arrangements and training facilities, might cost at least another £200,000. As a rough figure with which to estimate the impact of an infantry battalion on an African budget, it is safe to calculate on the basis of something between £500,000 and £600,000 a year. To run an air force is proportionately more expensive. Most African countries have therefore concentrated on air transport as a means of improving the mobility of their infantry, rather than as a system of air cover.[9]

Expenditure on military equipment tends to reflect political prestige rather than technical efficiency. It shows how closely the army represents the international status of a new state. For example, the police are always at a decided disadvantage in the reception of gifts from overseas governments. Capital investment in the police force requires far more in the way of recurrent costs, such as the provision of houses, police stations or posts, than the provision of hardware for the army. Even then armies frequently receive gifts of arms or technical equipment without making proper provision for their maintenance. A common fault is the failure to acquire spare parts. Ghana in 1967 received a hundred jeeps from Israel, without any spare parts. Already at that date it was doubtful whether it could mobilize more than 40 per cent of its lorries. The absence of spare parts and the weakness of the engineering workshops were frequently responsible for limiting the army's capability.

Relations between the army, the police, and the rest of the political community seem to have been governed in the first instance by the strength of the security forces as a lobby inside the state apparatus. Soldiers and policemen constituted a large sector in public employment. They possessed their own sense of

[9] For further details on air forces, see *Interavia*, August 1967, pp. 1305–1314; and Ross K. Baker, 'The Air Forces of Tropical Africa', *Air University Review*, Vol. XIX (2), January–February 1968, pp. 64–67.

cohesion, and could act almost as their own trades' union. All states were obliged to maintain their expensive services, and to attend to their demands. The francophone countries inherited the French system of military pensions, and therefore provided a government agency to meet the needs of retired soldiers, the *office des anciens combattants*. The former British Legion organizations in Ghana and Nigeria enjoyed official recognition, but not the same standing and importance.

The rest of the community tended to look upon soldiering and police work in terms of the social obligations of the extended family system. In Nigeria friends and relations used to subscribe to the bribe which was necessary to get a man into the army when the recruiting safari appeared in the village. If this were so, each soldier, when he received his salary, was naturally inclined to think in terms of paying back those who had supported him. The houses maintained by the colonial authorities for the expatriate officers, when they came into Nigerian hands, were frequently required to provide shelter for the extensive kinship group of the officer concerned. From the point of view of the peasantry, there seem to be only two alternatives in political action, either revolution, or a series of social adjustments by which each person and his family attempts to gain the most profit out of the system.

MILITARY STATUS AND POWER

In some countries, the peasantry has become accustomed to undisciplined soldiery. The individual soldier in the Congo, whatever his rank, between independence and the reconstruction of the army 1964, was able to enjoy almost unrivalled personal power over those with whom he was billeted, or against whom he was set to guard. Although often without regular pay, he could intimidate village people, and maintain a high standard of living. Even where the state apparatus has not been split by internal strife, as in the Congo, major units or individual groups of soldiers can theaten those around them, particularly if the latter belong to another tribe or region from that in which the army is recruited. The development of the army as a power base against the Kingdom of Buganda by the Uganda government was reflected in various bullying incidents, symbolized by the shooting of a crowd outside a night-club in Nakulabye by the police in December 1964. Baganda feelings against the Uganda army had been inflamed by the incident in October 1964 when an army lorry rammed a bus full of school children, killing several of them.

When an army is exposed to inter-tribal tensions of this kind, it is not surprising that junior officers, or even N.C.O.s, develop rather heady notions of personal aggrandisement. There are endless opportunities for the exercise of personal power when discipline on colonial lines collapses within the army. At the time of the second *coup* in Nigeria in July 1966, some of the most notorious reprisals taken against Ibos were effected under the command of a certain Warrant Officer who was in charge of the Ikeja Airport. In these conditions the men followed their 'natural leaders', and not their officers. Colonel Gowon was unable to guarantee that his orders would be obeyed. Colonial notions of hierarchy and discipline do not survive in a crisis which arouses strong feeling.

European notions of military professionalism survive wherever the army retains expatriate officers in key positions. But it is difficult to assess the extent of this professionalism, because operational skills are rarely tested. Kenya's war against the Somali *shifta* kept half the army deployed, but provided few opportunities for testing the stamina and strength of individual units. Some West African armies had their first experience of war as part of the United Nations Force in the Congo. Congolese conditions gave them ample opportunities for seeing the realities of mutiny. Conrad Nwawo, one of the Nigerian officers, was badly treated by Congolese soldiers. Colonel Hansen, a Ghanaian officer serving with the second battalion, was beaten up and left for dead by his own troops. Ghanaian units were placed under great strain, and were even defeated in Kasai in April 1961. For example, the Kalongist rebels mistook the tribal face-markings of Ghanaian northerners for those of their traditional enemies, the Luluas.

But perhaps the most important impact of the transfer of power on colonial standards of professionalism in African armies was the comparative neglect of training at the N.C.O. and technician level. Political conditions demanded the replacement of white officers by Africans, whereas the real strength of colonial troops lay in the technical skills of their N.C.O.s. The Engineers Support Units in the Gold Coast had trained such excellent mechanics that they were able to do without British other ranks immediately after World War II. Good technical men took longer to train than officers, particularly if the latter were sent on a short commission course. Sylvester Ogutu, who joined the K.A.R. in 1943, was not given command of the Kenya Field Engineering Company until 1967, although he had first been sent on a course to Britain for training in 1957. Some of the key technical posts were usually the last to be Africanized. For example, the arrangements made for the command of the Kenya Ordnance Depot were originally framed in terms which precluded an African Commanding Officer before 1970.

The difference between the rate of production of officers and that of other rank technicians represented the military equivalent of a universal phenomenon in the Civil Service. The 'transfer of power' required African permanent secretaries, not typists. This feature is very important. The creation of a successor state apparatus placed a great premium on the possession of western education of the kind usually associated with positions of administrative responsibility. To take over from the colonial administrator required the appropriate education 'ticket'. In military terms, when those with certificates of education could go forward for officer training, it was difficult to find sufficiently able technicians and N.C.O.s to take over fairly complicated clerical work and maintenance duty. The quartermaster-sergeant was harder to replace than the second lieutenant. Very little evidence is available on the standards of accounting procedure and ordnance supply which were maintained after the colonial powers had withdrawn. Expatriate training teams tended to think that one of their important roles was to lend a hand with clerical work and the maintenance of adequate supplies.

The criteria of achievement therefore encouraged by the transfer of power placed far greater emphasis on the exercise of administrative responsibility rather than upon technical skills. To be accepted for training as an officer in the army was primarily to secure a position of prestige, particularly in the early days of the mid-1950s, when Britain and France gave a very rigorous training to those whom they accepted as officers. The general officer formation course at either Sandhurst or Saint Cyr was usually followed by an intensive period of training in one of the professional schools. Ghanaian and Nigerian officers in particular, in anglophone Africa, were given wide varieties of experience. But however keen and proficient they became at their profession, after independence the conditions of officer provision tended to make them think of themselves more in terms of local criteria than in terms of metropolitan professionalism. In fact, as several French commentators pointed out, the officer cadre carried the burden of playing two contrasting roles, those played towards metropolitan audiences, and those played towards their own friends, relatives, and subordinates at home.

The greatest contrast was drawn for those who had been trained in the use of elaborate military equipment. If one had learnt to handle tanks, guns and armoured cars in Europe, as many had, it was frustrating to be placed in a position on returning home where much of the equipment was obsolescent or inadequately maintained. If only for this reason, French policy became much more selective than the British. It wished to avoid inculcating technical knowledge which could not easily be employed in African conditions. Trainees would of course become suspicious if they thought that courses were being limited for their benefit. Officers trained in Europe wished to be brought fully into all kinds of strategic discussions, and to be introduced to the latest weapons.

But on their return home, they were usually judged, not on their professional accomplishments, but on their social standing, prestige, and influence. They might be judged by their ability to help friends and relations, or by their acceptability to women. It is always said that the army of the Central African Republic was annoyed that the best women belonged to politicians. Military attachés, reporting on the sexual activities to African officers, often found it hard to adjust to societies where the possession of women is a sign of social status. Perhaps more important for the men themselves, army life gave them opportunities for self-improvement beyond any possible earlier hopes. Some careers already indicate that the army can be a stepping stone to other social roles. A. D. G. Nyirenda, who was dismissed from the Tanzanian army on its reconstruction in the Autumn of 1964, became an executive in the Shell Petroleum Company. A. R. Turay, who played a leading part in the first military take-over in Sierra Leone in 1967, voluntarily gave up his duties to continue studies at Cambridge, which had been originally stimulated by army experience.

Above all, a place in the army might present opportunities for political intrigue. For example, the rivalry between David Lansana and Ambrose Genda within the Sierra Leone officer corps, owed much more to grouping inside the Mende tribe than to professional considerations. Lansana objected to Genda's behaviour as acting Force Commander during his absence, and was able to get him 'kicked upstairs' into the diplomatic service in January 1966. On Genda's return to Sierra Leone after the military *coup* which had overthrown Lansana, he quickly became involved in new Mende intrigues, and was therefore again given a diplomatic post by the Chairman of the National Reformation Council.

One sign of the social standing conferred by the army was the developing convention that the diplomatic service provided a suitable base of privilege without great responsibility for those who were no longer required in the army. Brigadier Bassey of Nigeria was promoted to being Consul General in Fernando Po. David Hansen of Ghana was sent to be defence adviser to the High Commission in London. For Brigadier Ogundipe to have stayed in the Nigerian army would have been to court death. In the conditions prevailing in the time of the second Nigerian *coup*, the men would have only followed somebody with a northern ethnic background. Ogundipe became high commissioner in London.

The sudden and extensive expansion of an army naturally weakened the importance of professional criteria in judging the achievements of its officers. New professional criteria might be developed, but they were certainly not those of the former colonial army. The British and French armies had social traditions which emphasized officer 'qualities', which played an important part in maintaining orthodox professional standards during a period of sudden mobilization. But in Africa such qualities were irrelevant, and the expansion of an army left few people experienced in colonial methods to hand on a sense of tradition to new recruits. Perhaps the most important contrast between anglophone and francophone armies was that the former were subject to by far the greatest expansion (see Table Seven). The French army not only retained its influence over the armies of new francophone states, but also continued to lay emphasis on its own professional standards, and their validity in the training of Africans. Apart from Guinea, where conditions were exceptional no francophone army experienced sudden growth. The most important exception is that of Niger, where President Diori Hamani strengthened his regime with an expansion of the security forces; but this increase, from 900 to 1,900 in the army, with corresponding increases in the gendarmerie and *Garde Républicaine*, was small by anglophone standards. French training institutions have never been faced with the same problems of officer provision as those of Britain and Belgium. The collapse of professional standards under the impact of rapid change is largely an anglophone phenomenon. This can

TABLE SIX

ARMY COMMANDERS 1967

Country	Name	Date of Birth	Tribe	Other Rank Date of Enlist-ment	Officer Date of Commis-sion	Military Training Establishment
1. Enlisted in the ranks before 1939						
Dahomey	Soglo	1909	Fon	1931	1941	–
Mali	Sekou Traore	1911	Bambara	1929	1943	–
Senegal	Diallo	1911		1929	1943	–
Ivory Coast	Ouattara	1916	Tagouana	1936	1943	–
Upper Volta	Lamizana	1916	Samoko	1936	1949	–
Chad	Doumro	1919	Sara	1938	1955	–
C.A.R.	Bokassa	1921	Mbaka	1939	1958	–
2. Enlisted in the ranks between 1940 and 1949						
Kenya	Ndolo	1919	Kamba	1940	1961	–
Sierra Leone	Lansana	1922	Mende	1947	1952	–
Congo B.	Ebadei	1925	Bakouele	1946	1963	–
Niger	Belarabe	1925	Hausa	1944	1956	–
Uganda	Amin		Lugbara	1946	1961	–
Ghana	Kotaka	1926	Ewe	1947	1954	–
3. Enlisted in the ranks between 1950 and 1959						
Congo DR.	Mobutu	1930	Bangwandi	1950	1960	–
Togo	Eyadema	1935	Cambrai	1953	1963	–
4. Direct entry officers (or those with a few weeks in the ranks)						
Malagasy	Ramanantsoa	1906			1931	St. Cyr
Nigeria	Gowon	1934			1956	RMAS
Tanzania	Sarakikya	1934	Chagga		1961	RMAS
Mauritania	Mbareck	1935	Moor		1959	Off. de Reserve
Cameroun	Semengué	1935	Bassé Boulou		1957	St. Cyr
Burundi	Micombero	1940	Tutsi		1962	Belgian M.A.

easily be demonstrated by a comparison of anglophone and francophone military careers. A characteristic of the former are the blockages to promotion produced by the process of rapid officer creation. Some francophone states, such as Mauritania and Gabon, have still only Africanized their officer corps up to the level of major. There is a large gap in the Senegalese army between General Diallo at the top, and the young company commanders. The few holding intermediate ranks, perhaps significantly, have been given diplomatic posts or comparable jobs. In these conditions, subalterns can still see the way ahead open for them. It is also possible to continue to respect colonial professional standards.

Some of the significant differences between francophone and anglophone experience can be seen in a comparison of present day army commanders in the different spheres of influence. The position of the army commander may not be a very good index to the experience of the whole officer corps, because such a post is obviously politically sensitive, and subject to violent changes if there are also changes of regime. Nevertheless, those trained in the French tradition tend to belong to an older generation than their British trained counterparts, and therefore to have enjoyed a much longer period of military experience. In anglophone West Africa, the deaths of Ironsi and Kotaka, and the retirement of Lansana have brought an even younger generation to positions of responsibility. For example, Charles Blake, the Commander of the Sierra Leone army until the return to civilian rule, did not begin his military training until 1959, two years before his country's independence. His nearest francophone counterparts belonged to the two armies in French-speaking Africa, which significantly have had to be totally reconstructed. Semengué, the Commander in the Camerouns, who went to Saint Cyr from 1957 to 1959, is in charge of a force which grew rapidly to combat a serious internal rebellion and to meet the problems arising from the amalgamation of the eastern and western parts of the country, formerly under two separate colonial powers. Mbareck, the Commander of the Mauritanian army, represents a policy of constructing an army more in keeping with the Moorish and Muslim character of the country than could possibly have been provided from those Mauritanian members of the French army, who had largely been recruited from the negroid south and the borders of Senegal. But apart from these examples, where young people have risen quickly to the top, the commanders and chiefs of staff have tended to be

H

drawn from promoted non-commissioned officers rather than from direct officer entry.

The growth rates of armies in anglophone Africa give a clear indication of the strains which expansion placed upon their professional standards. It was almost impossible to sustain a growth rate of more than 15 per cent each year in the army without endangering the whole colonial apparatus of discipline and organization. Wherever British officers continued to exercise some influence, they usually attempted to restrain the forces pressing for an expansion of the army or the police. The war between Somalia and Kenya induced growth rates of slightly more than 15 per cent a year, but the social consequences of this expansion were tempered by the simple fact that the army had to be deployed in the field. Except in Tanzania, where the police force was increased in order to meet security threats during the period while the Tanzanian army was being reconstructed, police forces were unlikely to grow at a rate of more than 5 per cent a year. It is almost impossible to compare Congolese rates of expansion with those of anglophone Africa, because the operation carried out in the Congo was essentially that of reconstruction from existing forces, and not expansion.

The experience of the Sudan again seems to be different from that of the rest of English-speaking tropical Africa. The Sudanese drew up a three-year plan covering the years 1954–57, and appointed two boards, one to advise on the technical development of the army, and the other on its Sudanization. The implementation of the arrangements which they made was speeded up, first of all by the rebellion in the southern Sudan, and the need to expand the army rapidly, and secondly, by the decisions to foreshorten by one year the transitional arrangements for independence. But the whole Sudanese operation of expansion was essentially home-made. The motive for an almost three-fold expansion, from about 5,000 to about 15,000 men, was to make the Sudanese army independent of both the British and the Egyptian. The Sudanese Military College increased its output of officers ten fold from 10 to 100 a year. A few were sent abroad to other military colleges, but those trained at home met the most important needs. It also gave re-employment and temporary commissions to between 35 and 40 retired officers who had served with the Egyptian army during the 1920s. The condominium of Egypt and the Sudan left a legacy of military experience which could be exploited in a crisis. There was nothing comparable in the rest of tropical Africa.

TABLE SEVEN

SECURITY FORCES
Estimated Growth Rates

	Army				Police		
	Growth ratio		Years covered	Annual growth rate %	Growth ratio		Years covered	Annual growth rate %
Kenya	1967	5,000	4	18·9	1967	12,123	4	nil
	1963	2,500			1963	12,124		
Uganda	1967	7,000	5	48	1967	7,392	5	5·4
	1962	1,000			1962	5,692		
Tanzania	disbanded and reformed*				1967	10,658	6	11
					1961	5,700		
Malawi	1967	10,86	3	13·1	1967	3,031	3	4·9
	1964	750			1964	2,624		
Zambia	1967	3,200	3	13·3	1967	7,000	3	6
	1964	2,200			1964	5,880		
Ghana	1967	14,000	7	10·4	1967	14,114	10	8·5
	1960	7,000			1957	6,271		
Sierra	1967	1,200	6	3·1	1967	2,493	6	0·6
Leone	1961	1,000			1961	2,402		
Nigeria	1966	12,000	6	7	1967	17,000	7	4·6
(before coup)	1960	8,000			1960	12,417		

* 2,000 to 5,000 including Zanzibar forces from 1961 to 1967.

Uganda experienced the most fantastic military growth rate in the whole continent. It expanded its army at a rate of well over 40 per cent a year without being able to fall back upon a large reservoir of trained manpower. The Uganda government thought this necessary, not only to meet the growing security threats caused by refugees from the Sudan, the Congo and Rwanda, but also to provide protection against possible open rebellion in Buganda. British contingency planning had recommended that at least four battalions were necessary to maintain order in Buganda, if a violent uprising took place. The Uganda army sustained this expansion only at the expense of regular purges – it also probably has the highest rate of officer dismissal in the continent – and of constant competition between the N.C.O.s and the officers. After the successful operations against Buganda in 1966, it was able to settle down with a formation of two brigades, one of two battalions and the other of three battalions, with training teams from Israel, Russia, and China.

The Russians were largely concentrated in the Air Base built outside Buganda in the north, at Gulu. Uganda's problems represented in an acute form the difficulties which were found elsewhere.

Soldiers were regarded as privileged members of the community; expansion merely emphasized certain aspects of this élite status. Peter Lloyd in describing the activities of African élites has divided the tensions which develop into three categories; first, there may be differences based on ethnic origins; secondly, differences of generation; and thirdly, differences based upon functional distinctions,[10] such as those performing general and those performing technical duties. In most African armies the first two kinds of difference seem the most important. As has been explained above, the social standing of soldiers seems more significant than their actual functions.

The conventions of colonial days which separated the army from the rest of the community were broken down, precisely because the officer corps tended to be subject to the same tensions as civilian élites, and as equally confused as they were by conflicting notions of personal success. In one sense, the regime in power was not obliged to take measures which would give it control over the army; the political community recolonized it. The army became the battleground for warring factions if large sections of the community found it impossible to identify with the regime. In these conditions, it is not surprising that the army's sense of professionalism is significantly lowered. Young officers in particular, who have all received their commissions since independence, have barely had time to assimilate a sense of military tradition, especially if that tradition has been under attack.

As a general rule, there are three principal levels in the officer corps of each army. The first category contains few in number and is largely French-speaking. It consists of those who had full officer status before 1955. They are such venerable figures as General Ramanantsoa, the Commander of the Malagasy army, who was at Saint Cyr from 1931–33, and General Ankrah, the Chairman of the Ghanaian National Liberation Council, who was one of the first Africans to receive the Queen's Commission. The second category consists of promoted N.C.O.s. As has been shown above, this type of officer predominates among African commanders and chiefs of staff, because they have the greatest military experience. But none of them acquired full officer status

[10] Lloyd, *op. cit.*, pp. 14–15.

until either just before or just after independence. The third category is by far the largest and the most vocal, and consists of all those who have been commissioned through a direct entry system. They have all received more formal education than either of the other two categories. They sometimes contain men who are starting a new career, particularly in those expanding armies which are desperately short of officer material. For example, among the thirty officer cadets sent to Ghana by the Minister of Defence in Uganda in 1965, there were several former primary school-teachers, an engineering assistant from the Public Works Department, and a clerk from the Ministry of Regional Administrations.[11] But the more usual type of officer cadet enters the army directly from school through the machinery which was established by the colonial authorities as a method of officer selection. In anglophone Africa, the most distinguished group of officers were those selected by the West Africa selection Board, and sent on the special training course at Teshie in Ghana. The latter consisted of 180 men in thirteen separate entries between 1953 and 1960.[12] In francophone Africa, such officers were the products of the leading military schools, such as the *Ecole Leclerc* at Brazzaville, and the Military School at Bingerville.

Both the British and the French army concentrated on giving a sense of military tradition to schoolboys, but British plans in particular were overtaken by events. The special instruction which they provided was designed to provide the armies with intelligent N.C.O.s and technicians as well as officers. But the time scale of these operations had to be telescoped to meet the demands of Africanization. The establishment of boys' companies in West Africa, which had a 14-year-old entry, was delayed because the War Office emphasized that the colonies themselves must bear the whole cost. Initially, only the Gold Coast felt able to do this. It formed the first boys' company in 1952; Nigeria followed in 1953. The latter in 1955 also created cadet units in certain selected colleges and secondary schools. The East Africa Command equivalent was the Junior Leader Company, formed in Nairobi in 1957, with 45 boys from the whole of East Africa, although 20 of them were Kamba, from Kenya. The most ambitious project of this kind began too late to have any real impact on the problems facing

[11] See *The Square*, Ghana Military Academy Journal 1965, pp. 8–11.
[12] The Teshie 'old boys' (88 Nigerians, 82 Ghanaians, and 10 Sierra Leoneans) provide important personal links between the three armies.

a new country immediately after independence. The Sierra Leone Military Forces Secondary School was not started until 1960, soon after Brigadier Blackie took command of the army. This institution, unlike the others in anglophone Africa, was run by the army and the Ministry of Education jointly, and therefore had civilian teachers, although the boys wore military uniform. It was highly selective, taking 16 boys aged between 13 and 14 a year for a full five-year academic training course leading to the General Certificate of Education. But the whole political situation had been transformed by the time the first year's entry was ready to pass into the army. All these schemes reflect the army's desire to begin with the young and the well-educated.

All the new armies, immediately after independence, appear to have experienced some difficulty in reconciling the outlooks of the second and third category of officer. The promoted N.C.O.s who had considerable military experience under colonial officers, were naturally prejudiced against their younger direct-entry colleagues. The Uganda mutiny of January 1964, said to have been led by an Education Corps N.C.O., suggests that tensions between experienced and educated officers constitutes a grave threat to the colonial tradition of discipline. Even if there had been no Zanzibar Revolution to spark off mutiny in the minds of the soldiers, the Uganda army at that time had reached a very delicate point in its development. The mutiny took place less than six weeks after the return of eight officers from the British Cadet School at Mons. The direct entry for the first time tipped the balance in the officer corps against the former N.C.O.s. The latter numbered only 16, joined by 21 direct-entry officers. The mutiny was touched off by the Minister's signal announcing revised pay-scales for N.C.O.s., without an equivalent scale for the other ranks, although the latter was supposed to be forthcoming. The Uganda army under Amin's command has continued to show suspicion of direct-entry officers. The first Ugandan cadet at Sandhurst, Karugaba, was also among the first to be dismissed.

Education provision and political necessity led to the creation in East Africa of a half-and-half rank known as the *effendi*.[13] Those promoted to this rank, who were former N.C.Os, were usually given full regular commissions after 1961, when it became necessary to provide regular officers quickly. But their very existence had underlined the fact that a position in the new

[13] See above, pp. 42–43.

state apparatus depended upon formal educational qualifications rather than upon professional experience. Former *effendis* provided the core of the new Kenyan army. The KAR Battalions in Kenya had received a high proportion of these men – for example, 12 out of the first 18 appointed in 1957. By the summer of 1966 more than 60 per cent of those holding the rank of major or above in the Kenya army had been *effendis*. At the same date, Malawi was in a comparable position, although the Nyasa battalion does not appear to have had any *effendis*. But a similar proportion of promoted N.C.O.s provided the basis of the platoon command structure.

The differences of opinion between the experienced and the educated were partly due to age, and partly due to genuinely different methods of exercising authority. Under the colonial power, the N.C.O. had enjoyed a rather unique position, particularly if he were exercising the informal authority of his tribe over its members. Discipline in East Africa was maintained not by expatriate officers giving orders, but through the traditional method of discussion, palavers or *barazas*, over which the senior N.C.O. usually presided. The direct-entry officer cadet could only use, in the first instance, expatriate methods of exercising authority, and could not necessarily expect the N.C.O.s to give him the traditional deference and support.

When did conflicts between ethnic groups become more important than those between age groups, or between people of different educational background? All armies became conscious of ethnic divisions within the officer corps whenever political competition among civilians inflamed personal rivalries to such an extent that the whole of society was involved. If the whole army, both officers and men, came largely from one particular ethnic group, as in Uganda, dissident ethnic elements inside the army which were in a minority could easily be removed. The Teso and Bantu group inside the Uganda army could only have succeeded if it had struck first.

But the more normal situation was for competing groups to attempt some kind of ethnic balance, as in appointments to the civil service. This principle of course is directly contrary to European notions of professionalism, yet societies composed of many different groups find in such a principle some method for controlling the institutions of the state, and for ensuring that they are representative. If there are strong rivalries between two or three major power groups, then there may be certain personal advantages in belonging to a minority tribe. Nigeria laid down a strict quota system for the recruitment of officer cadets. This was on a fifty-fifty basis, for north and south, with 50 cadets from the north as against 25 from the east and 25 from the west. The alternative to such a system, as was amply demonstrated in the collapse of recruiting methods after the second *coup* in Nigeria, was a kind of confederation of regional forces based upon local recruiting. After independence, Kenya deliberately followed a policy of trying to make the army more representative. In terms of the officer corps, this shifted the emphasis away from the Kamba, and brought in far more Kikuyu. By 1967, the Kikuyu had as many officers as the Kamba, and the army was broadly representative. The number of Nandi and Kipsigis officers whom the British had considered to be suitable warriors, were cut down to the proper proportion. The commanding officers of the three Kenya battalions were also appointed on this ethnic balance principle; one Kamba, one Kikuyu, and one Nandi or Kipsigis. The second-in-command usually came from a minority tribe. The Luhya, who formed an important element in the police, were poorly represented in the army.

TABLE EIGHT

KENYA: TRIBAL BALANCES
BY PERCENTAGES

Tribe	1962 Census	1962 Police Force	1966 Army Officer Corps
Kikuyu	19·2	11·2	22·7
Luo	13·9	8·5	10·3
Luhya	12·9	16·5	0·4
Kamba	11·0	9·8	28·0
Kipsigis	4·0	7·6	2·8
Nandi	2·0	7·4	4·1
Total	63·0	61·0	68·3

Kenya settled down to this principle of balance very quickly, because the whole of its politics before independence had been dominated by tribal divisions. In Zambia, in contrast, tribal divisions within the United National Independence Party (UNIP) did not begin to show themselves until 1966, when a certain polarization began to develop between Bemba on the one hand, and the Barotse and their associates on the other. Until then, the government allowed British expatriate officers to run an officer selection board based on a merit system. When the Zambian government began to make enquiries, it discovered that the Bemba were heavily under-represented in the officer corps. Expatriate advisers, British in the army and Israeli in the youth service, continued training schemes in spite of hostility between warring factions which came into the open at the party conference in August 1967.

It seems important the officer corps at least should be roughly representative of the constituent elements. Some regimes maintain a deliberate imbalance. For example, the Government of Uganda can only trust an army that is dominated by Nilotics. Elsewhere, accidental imbalances are found as a result of the different patterns of educational experience between regions of the same country, or of different family traditions and associations. The ethnic origins of the officer corps assume a new importance in conditions of extreme political tension. Ironically, the more a government has striven to make its officer corps representative of the new nation, the more it makes its army vulnerable to complete collapse if the coalition of interests in the civilian order also breaks down. One of the principal consequences of colonial patterns of recruitment was that the officers and the other ranks tended to come from different parts of the country. Wherever direct officer entry has been encouraged, the officer corps came from those areas with the best secondary school provision.

The Ghanaian officer corps was much more out of balance with the population than that of the Nigerian army. Over half those above the rank of major in Ghana came from the small coastal tribes, Ga and Fanti, whereas the great bulk of the men were recruited from the poorer areas of the former Northern Territory (see Table Nine). Yet the Ghanaian army was able to act together in order to overthrow the Nkrumah regime, while the Nigerian army collapsed under the strains of the federal system. In Nigeria, where the officer corps was much better balanced because of the quota system, southern discontent with the dominance of the north in the federal coalition led to a plot inside the army; and northern discontent with the first military regime produced the second counter-*coup*. It will probably never be known how much, if at all, General Ironsi was involved in the first *coup* in Nigeria, but the contrast between his behaviour as a professional soldier before and after it seems to be quite startling. Before the first *coup* destroyed the structure of civilian competition, Ironsi displayed considerable skill in balancing the different interests within the army, particularly in

TABLE NINE

THE GHANAIAN ARMY HIGH COMMAND: 1967

Ethnic Origins

Rank	Ga	Fanti	Ashanti	Northern	Ewe	Other
Generals	Ankrah (52) Bruce (43)	Ocran (38)			Kotaka (43) (Killed April, 1967)	
Brigadiers	Crabbe (39)		Afrifa (31)		Amenu (38)	
Colonels	Slater (38) Laryea (41) Adjeitey Addo (44) Addy (41)	Mensah-Brown Yarboi (41)			Tevie (38) Kattah (35) Quaye (43)	Hassan* Ewa (38) Sanni-Thomas (40) Lartey (43)
Lieutenant Colonels	Ashitey*	Coker-Appiah Dontoh Acquah J. R. K. Tachie-Menson Bernasco Appiah H. A.	Asafu-Adjaye (41) Acheampong	Zanlerigu* (35) Kuti*		Okai(33) Koranteng Asare Nyante Twum-Barimah Assassie*
Majors	Tetteh Kotei	Acquah S. K.* Baidoo Erskine Parker-Yarney	Oduro	Hamidu Kabore Achaab*	Tay	Akuffo Asante* Osei-Owusu
Total: 52 =	11	13	4	5	6	13

* Retired for political reasons   Figures in brackets = age of those with regular commissions before independence.

reconciling the conflicting claims of the two Brigadiers, Maima-
lari and Ademulegun. The latter was widely acknowledged to
be more intelligent than himself. But as soon as he was thrust
into a position of power by the first *coup*, he rapidly became
involved in promoting the ambitions of people from his own
eastern region, and his own tribe, the Ibos. Federal publications
issued after the second *coup* have emphasized how the promotions which he made in April 1966 included 18 Ibo officers
out of the 21 who met with his approval. The fact that the
officers came largely from the south, and the men from the
north was important in Nigeria when a federal government
combining the interests of two parts was under strain. But in
Ghana, it did not attract the same significance, because the
Ghanaian south never felt itself to be overwhelmed by the north,
and there was no federal system to accentuate regional interests.
The south itself had a different kind of inter-ethnic tension,
partly because of the Ewe tribe, which straddled the eastern
border with Togo.

It looks as if the army is more likely to succumb to the
influence of the values expressed by the political community,
than to create and diffuse new concepts of national identity.
Some armies have been accused of being much more inclined to
support the interests of outside powers than of their own people.
Fitch and Oppenheimer, in their Marxist critique of Ghana
after the *coup*, implied that the army there retained its coherence because it saw itself as the protector of the capital
investments made by European firms.[14] Differences of ethnic
origin lose their significance if the army stays close to colonialist
standards! But it is hard to regard the army as an instrument of
the 'ruling classes' if there is a possibility that both military and
civilian élites will divide on communal lines. When faced with a
political crisis, the army tends to split along the same lines as the
political community, unless it is already closely identified with
one section, or is able to retain a certain professional aloofness,
because it relies heavily upon foreign resources.

OVERSEAS AID

How far does the presence of overseas military assistance
separate security forces from the communities with which they
are involved? Is it true that the army may continue to represent

[14] B. Fitch and M. Oppenheimer, 'Ghana: End of an Illusion', *Monthly Review*, Vol. 18, No. 3, July–August 1966.

the presence of the former colonial power? As was explained in the second chapter, the army may appear to be a symbol of the former colonial authority, and as such to be less than responsive to the needs of the new regime. International recognition may seem more important for the army than for the regime itself. Military regimes, when they have been established, are usually conscious that ties with the former metropolitan power, or with other great powers in the world make it much easier for them to secure recognition. They may not necessarily be directly responsive to the interests of outside powers. It is frequently alleged that the CIA was implicated in the Congolese *coup* of 1965. The army's interpretation of its own interest may seem to coincide with that of the western powers. No interpretation of the process of the transfer of power can avoid asking questions about the possibility that the security forces might collectively appear more sensitive to the forces of international politics than to the ambitions of their own governments.

The sensitivity of security forces to the needs of the community is a separate subject for the next chapter. It is easier to test the responsiveness of a given body of men to the defence of a particular regime. Those who have attempted to formulate general hypotheses on a world-wide scale usually relate the quickness of response to the origin of the resources which the army consumes. As has been explained above, the army, much more easily than the police, can rely for a significant proportion of its resources on overseas technical assistance. The model which several theorists have postulated to explain this significance is based on the idea that there can be a kind of 'exchange of services' between a government and its army. This puts the defence of a regime on a par with the marketing of goods. At first sight, the speed with which an army jumps to the defence of a regime depends on the degree to which its maintenance comes from domestic resources. Charles Wolf has formulated several hypotheses along these lines;[15] Moshe Lissak has applied the idea of Burmese conditions,[16] but the only area of the world on which there is enough evidence to work is Latin America. In Africa, hypotheses framed on these lines are much more difficult to prove.

[15] 'The Political Effects of Military Programs', *Orbis*, VIII (4), Winter 1965.
[16] 'Social Change, Mobilization, and Exchange of Services between the Military Establishment and the Civil Society: the Burmese case', *Economic Development and Cultural Change*, XIII (1), Part I, October 1964.

Most regimes are reluctant to accept a defence system which is purely mercenary. The ethos of the successor state apparatus is that it should rely upon new nationalist loyalties. European mercenaries have of course been frequently employed, particularly in civil war conditions, as in Nigeria and Biafra. They have the value of being easily dismissed, unless they mutiny, as in the Congo.

There are obviously different degrees of dependence on outside resources. A major power can supply two basic kinds of assistance, first, equipment, and second, facilities for training. There is a third type of assistance which is more controversial, the maintenance of a base inside the territory itself. Bases mean the presence of foreign troops on African soil. Only France has consistently followed this pattern of aid-giving, although its commitments have been greatly reduced since 1964 and 1965.

Military assistance in equipment and training seems to fall into certain recognized patterns. Equipment given to African armies may be extremely lavish, as in Ethiopia, or it may be confined to certain crack units. The politics of placing defence contracts can affect the situation very strongly. Either the country retains the same basic equipment from the same source, or there is a diversification of equipment from different overseas donors or suppliers. Training facilities are usually either places allotted in colleges in Europe or America, or training teams sent to the host country. The spectrum therefore runs from fairly total dependence on one hand, to a strong bargaining position on the other. Michael Bell's Adelphi paper on military assistance shows the range of possibilities.[17] Most of the francophone states listed there accept French training teams and French equipment throughout. Those states which are a little more independent, such as the Sudan or Tanzania, retain fairly standard patterns of equipment from overseas, but diversify their training system and advice. Few states are in the happy position of not being dependent on outside powers for the re-equipment of certain units, or the training of specialist technicians. A country such as Ghana, which has deliberately diversified its pattern of aid acceptance, may of course stand in a different position with each of the powers that help it.

The donors themselves are naturally not driven by objective assessments of the needs of each government. They are much

[17] M. J. V. Bell, *Military Assistance to Independent African States*, Adelphi Paper No. 15 (London: Institute for Strategic Studies, 1964).

more concerned to see how their own assessments of their own advantage work out in the new post-colonial context of security. There is a general willingness to support regimes which continue to show sympathy for a country's foreign policy. Israel's investment of time and energy in aid to Africa must be seen as part of its campaign for votes in the United Nations. A return on diplomatic capital requires a certain flexibility of manner. West Germans, for example, although skilful in gaining trade, have found it hard to adapt to African military customs. The German training teams with air forces of Tanzania and Nigeria were not popular. The great powers, the United States and Russia, now appear anxious to avoid deep involvement in African affairs, particularly if such an involvement might extend the field of conflict.

The former colonial powers are placed in a rather obviously different position. Belgium, Britain, and France, having created these armies, are under certain obligations to maintain them. It is usually a break in the colonial structure of relations that admits new powers into the military assistance field. Philippe Decraene, in an assessment of United States policy, published in January 1967, demonstrated that the inconsistency of supporting opposing regimes, such as those of Guinea and the Ivory Coast, could only be justified on the general principle that any vacuum ought to be filled.[18] The United States came to the assistance of Mali in 1961, really its first important venture in Africa outside Ethiopia, when the French withdrew. Russia had similarly come to the aid of Guinea in 1958. The strains between Britain and Uganda in 1963–64 provided the opportunity for Israeli assistance; those between Britain and Tanzania, led the latter to call upon Canadian assistance in 1964. Before that date, British officers had made a desperate effort to retain their privileged position in East Africa, even to the extent of accepting certain humiliations, such as being by-passed by the ministries of defence concerned. The former colonial powers labour under a certain handicap, because the successor state apparatus is in part their own creation, and therefore those who hold public office immediately after independence enjoy a certain legitimacy in the eyes of their former masters, which no other regimes can enjoy. Other powers are in a stronger position to maintain informal relations with possible successors to the existing regime. But they are all exposed to allegations of conspiracy. In November 1964 the United States

[18] *Le Monde*, 4, 5, and 6 January, 1967.

was accused of plotting to overthrow the Tanzanian government from a base in the Congo.

Military assistance schemes provide opportunities for sponsors other than the new states themselves. The contrast between those armies which result from the transfer of power, and other military organizations involved in political fighting, can be seen in the different emphases placed on training and equipment in the two situations. Nkrumah's reception of freedom fighters into special training camps inside Ghana, where they received instruction from Chinese training teams, was based upon the principle that havoc could be caused in the political system of an unfriendly regime by a few men with a few primitive weapons. The Chinese in their aid to the revolutionary movements in the Congo, Channelled largely through Burundi or through Congo (Brazzaville), concentrated on guerrilla methods.[19] In Tanzania, the Chinese advisers were deliberately concentrated in the south, because of the aid which the army was giving to the liberation movement in Mozambique. Only the Chinese mission to Uganda fails to fit into this pattern. The supply of arms by outside powers appears to be more important in sustaining a civil war than in starting it. Wherever the successor state apparatus breaks down, it is usually possible to find the necessary arms from existing stocks.

The war in Nigeria between the federal authorities and the secessionist regime of Biafra is sustained by foreign supplies of arms and even mercenaries. Air power is an important psychological weapon. Biafra appears to have relied on an arms dealer in Paris whose weapons are ferried by air through Lisbon and the Portuguese controlled air-route – Lisbon, Bissau, and Sao Tome. It was often rumoured that European businessmen behind the SAFRAP (*Société Anonyme Française de Recherches et d'eploitation de Pétrole*) organization, rivals with Shell-BP for Eastern Nigerian oil, supplied the credit. The Federal authorities accepted delivery of Russian and Czech aircraft, and are believed to have employed Egyptian pilots as well as British and South African mercenaries to fly them.

Those who designed the process for transferring powers to new governments did not anticipate the range of possibilities which the rise of other sponsoring organizations would create. In the eyes of the former colonial powers, the major defence of

[19] P. Alexandre, 'Note on the Activities of the Communist Powers in French Speaking Africa', *East–West Confrontation in Africa* (The Hague, 1966).

any new regime was not the speed and efficiency of its security forces, at least not against external security threats, but the willingness of those in responsibility inside the army or the police force, as well as other positions in the public service, not to alter the existing balance of power. The transfer of power was based on the assumption that it need not necessarily alter the strategic significance of the area. Any regime which rejects this assumption was admitting too many unknown factors into the situation.

Military intelligence for powers outside Africa has therefore become largely a matter of reporting upon the reliability of given individuals, or on the fragility of the political system. The French might be able to subsume such intelligence under the pattern of co-operation and technical assistance established within the French community; the British to place their activities within a system of Commonwealth relations. But any violent change of regime had implications for the acceptability of the state to a whole range of international agencies. Zanzibar, the only place to experience a real revolution, avoided the essential difficulties by its union with Tanganyika, although this union has never been fully implemented, even to the extent of retaining two systems of army command, and virtually two defence forces. The union government of Tanzania faced the difficulty of having representatives from two opposing systems, such as east and west Germany, in its two halves. The Brazzaville regime which replaced that of Foulbert Youlon in 1963 retained a certain degree of international acceptability in spite of its 'left-wing' character, because the French trained army were sympathetic to the change. The defence agreements signed with France by the majority of francophone states constituted almost an international recognition system in themselves. The clauses which gave France the opportunity of intervening enabled it to exercise a kind of veto power. The intervention of French troops in February 1964 in Gabon was the most notorious incident in this set of relationships, but it was by no means the only move made by the former metropolitan power. Movements of French troops, such as those to the Central African Republic in 1967, have an important psychological affect on the local situation. They had obviously been important in determining the course of events in Chad and Niger in 1963. In certain conditions the French President was in a position of being able to approve or disapprove of a particular change of regime. It is frequently alleged that although the French Government conceded to the need for military regimes in Upper Volta and Dahomey in 1966, they expressed strong feelings of disapproval against the change in the Central African Republic.

The Organization of African Unity (OAU), established in 1963, largely under Nkrumah's inspiration, has never enjoyed sufficient cohesion to maintain its own system of recognition, if there are obviously violent changes of regime. Its acceptance of the new Ghanaian regime in 1966, after considerable manœuvre among those states which objected to the trend of events in Ghana, exposed its major weakness. Its major successors have nearly all been in the field of support for liberation movements in Southern Africa against the Portuguese or the regime of the Union of South Africa. But it had to abandon any attempt to organize concerted resistance inside Rhodesia after the declaration of independence by the Smith regime in 1965. The proposal to set up a war command, with its own funds supplied by the member states, first discussed at the meeting in Kinshasa in 1967, was also primarily concerned with the situation in Southern Africa.[20] Inter-state Pan-African co-operation at the military assistance level has largely been on a bilateral basis, and not on a regional or continental basis. Even where there are defence pacts, as in East Africa, co-operation in the fields of equipment and training seems difficult to effect. Malawi and Zambia sent officer cadets for training in East Africa, but found that in some ways it was politically less dangerous to send them to England itself. The rapid Africanization programme in Kenya did not fit in with the Central African situation, or with their government's view of progress in this direction. The East African states have sent officer cadets to Ethiopia and the Sudan for training, but not on any large scale. Although it is easy for any particular regime to reject advice from a single military source, its former colonial master, it remains difficult to avoid the consequences of the whole pattern of equipment, practices, and law, laid down during the colonial period.

An army can therefore be regarded as an organization which maintains a certain distance from the community in which it operates, when its training and equipment seem to have been deliberately designed to improve its acceptability to outside powers. If a regime depends on the possible intervention of an outside power in internal security problems, as many francophone states do, its own security forces must be compatible with

[20] *The Times*, 12 September, 1967.

I

those of its chief assistant. The French have emphasized this in the pattern of joint manœuvres which they have built up since the defence agreements were signed in the period 1960–63. Although the Ivory Coast, manœuvres in 1967 demonstrated the weakness of French forces of intervention, particularly their dependence on air transport facilities, they represented the principle of acceptability in its most direct form.[21] The flurry of questions about the absence of representatives from Tanzania and Uganda at the Commonwealth Defence Study, which reviewed British experience of counter-insurgency operations between 1950 and 1966, indicated the sensitivity of British chiefs of staff to the presence of African officers who had Chinese advisers.[22] The system of co-operation between a mother-country and its former colonies depended not only on a common language, a common set of equipment, and a common set of training methods, but also upon the persistence of a political climate in which officers could continue to use the same set of assumptions. If staff college discussions allowed officers to talk to each other within their normal professional frame of reference, then African participants were trusted to support the existing balance of power.

Such a sense of confidence led to a greater emphasis being placed upon the training function than upon the equipment function in determining the levels of acceptability. The British could train Sierra Leone troops with Israeli guns; the Americans could effectively train crack units in the army of Mali with Russian equipment. Many people concerned with military assistance programmes believed that they were dealing with conditions where a few bullets or the possession of small arms could affect a whole political system, and that therefore the orientation of the troops was more important than their technical proficiency. Training programmes, particularly if they involved visits by African candidates to institutions in Europe or America, were considered the surest way of maintaining long-term ties with the African military. In the period of reappraisal of American policy following the Draper Report of 1952,[23] United States army officers even went as far as to debate whether or not democratic values could be instilled in those who accepted American training facilities. The French tended to

[21] *Le Monde*, September 20, 1967.
[22] *The Times*, August 18, 1967.
[23] William H. Draper, *Report of the U.S. Special Representative in Europe to the President* (Washington: Government Printer, 1952).

judge the viability of armies according to the proportion of officers and men who had absorbed the main tenets of French culture. The British, in comparing their relationships with West Africa and with East Africa, were struck by the degree to which educational standards in West Africa had permitted Nigerian and Ghanaian officers to absorb British administrative procedures in far greater depth than any of their East African counterparts.

The Belgian record in the training sphere was the least consistent; the French the most extensive. Because of the many changes of Congolese policy, and of the need to co-ordinate its activities with those of other powers in the Congo, Belgium was not really able to diversify the kind of assistance which it gave to Congolese military forces until 1966 and 1967. By this time the relationships between Congo and Belgium were dominated by the strains over the nationalization of the *Union Minière,* and Belgium was again compelled to withdraw a great deal of its assistance. At any given point in time between 1964 and 1967, there were barely more than 100 or so soldiers of all kinds from the Congo, Ruanda, and Burundi training in Belgium. The equivalent figure for trainees from the francophone states in France was between 1,000 and 2,000. It is said that some 2,600 men were trained in France from francophone Africa between 1960 and 1964.

French commitment to a policy of bases and defence agreements meant a strong flow in the reverse direction, Frenchmen working in Africa. While the Belgians in 1964 had about 500 soldiers of all kinds working within their former African territories, the French had over 11,000 men scattered throughout francophone Africa. Even after the decision to cut down on these commitments and to withdraw a large number of troops, the presence of Frenchmen in the key bases at Dakar, Fort Lamy, and Diego Suarez continued to swell the numbers. By November 1966 there were about 4,000 soldiers of different kinds, 1,400 regulars, 2,100 conscripts, and others who had retired or were carrying out civilian duties.

The figures for British personnel in anglophone Africa fluctuated according to the ups and downs of diplomatic relations. The chief bases for British training teams were to be found in Kenya, Zambia, and Ghana, with a smaller contingent in Malawi. The largest of these contingents was the 150 man training team in Kenya in 1964. The British made a distinction between officers on loan and officers on contract which did not apply elsewhere. Contract officers formed a considerable portion of the officer corps in Zambia and Malawi.

The presence of training teams represented a change of policy which was common to all former colonial powers. For speed and cheapness, particularly in officer provision, the new regimes preferred to accept foreign advisers on their own soil, rather than send their own men to metropolitan institutions. Even the French changed the main slant of their policy. Francophone states were encouraged to establish their own military academies, and to send only the best pupils from these for training in France. Israel was particularly good at mounting on-the-spot courses at short notice.[24] Although this technique had been originally developed in such fields as youth leadership and agricultural extension work, it could easily be applied to military training, or to police work. For example, in the summer of 1965, Israel sent several teachers of public administration to Tanzania in order to train the local police force.

The development of military academies in Africa itself was an excellent opportunity to reconsider the whole curriculum of training for officers. It was no longer necessary to fit into the metropolitan system of provision. Neither the British nor the French had arranged special courses, indeed, both insisted that African candidates should be split up and divided with other cadets from overseas, and with British or French colleagues. The British made a single exception to this rule when they allowed a full batch of Kenyans to pass through the Mons Officer Cadet School as a single platoon in 1964. Although it was challenging to design courses more appropriate to African needs, expatriate advisers tended to discourage local institutions, because they doubted whether there would be enough candidates to warrant them, as soon as the rapid expansion which took place after independence had been completed. Political pressures to create local institutions were combined with the idea that military training was not necessarily of value to the army alone. Furthermore, potential army officers might well benefit from the experience of being trained alongside other members of the state apparatus, such as senior civil servants, policemen, or senior party officials. The design of new curriculum was some indication of the orientation of the regime in power.

Wherever a militant party had decided to establish an ideological training school, or its equivalent, there was naturally

[24] See *Shalom* (Alumni Bulletin of Israel-trained Students), No. 8, May 1965, pp. 48–56.

considerable pressure for army officers to participate. One of the first moves made by President Nkrumah after the departure of British officers in the Ghanaian army was to create an armed forces bureau which was intended to organize seminars within the army at the staff officer level. He also attempted in 1963 and 1964 to induce army officers to accept courses in party ideology at the Winneba Ideological Institute, but the Ghanaian army was able to resist these attentions. To integrate the army into the ruling party structure required a more thorough-going system, such as that practised in Guinea and Mali. The first national seminar for army officers and N.C.O.s in Mali was held in October 1963. Mali opened its own military academy with local instructors in 1962, giving a full two-year course to N.C.O.s with ten years schooling or the equivalent. Appointments and promotions depend to some extent in these cases upon party reliability. Several party organizations, such as TANU in Tanzania, have been used as a basis for recruitment into the public service. Party branches, or members of Parliament, were asked to nominate candidates for the process of selection. This device was also used in Kenya when the National Youth Service was created. This method of approach makes it possible for the army or other branches of the public service to be considered fairly representative of all interests in the country, but it does not necessarily imbue those at the top with a common sense of purpose.

Perhaps the most successful model in francophone Africa of a training institution which attempted to combine both the army and other services as well as a system of indoctrination, is the military school run by the Malagasy Republic. The first candidates were selected for a three year course in 1965. They were told at its beginning that their training would be primarily for the three arms of the security services, first the army, second the gendarmerie, and thirdly the *service civique*, and that places in France for further training would be reserved for the few who were considered the best. It was also emphasized under this scheme that future posts in the higher ranks of the Civil Service would be reserved for men with this type of background, who had had a period of military training and a period of service in the security forces. This institution therefore, began with a general ethos of public service in all its branches.

The countries of British Africa have been less adventurous in this respect, or at least have tried to keep their military training separate from the rest of the public services. Ghana began a two year officer training course at the school in Teshie, modelled on the Royal Military Academy at Sandhurst. The first Ghanaian instructor, David Asare, was appointed in January 1960, and the first intake began work in April 1960. In fact the courses taken by this intake and its successor were foreshortened in order to provide platoon commanders for the Ghanaianization of the army which took place in the autumn of 1961. The course was designed for an intake of about 30 each year, although a larger number were taken in some years, particularly in the years immediately after 1961 when the air force was also being included in the same scheme. The officer training course due to begin in Zambia in 1968 appears to have been designed on similar lines. It is not clear whether the Tanzanian course at Arusha, which was designed by a Canadian training team, will be related to other branches of the public service.

One of the difficulties of instituting staff college courses in local academies was the absence of any adequate studies of local conflicts, which could provide the students with appropriate syndicate work. In anglophone Africa, the first moves to remedy the situation were not made until January 1963, when Colonel Plummer was sent to the Sudan in order to prepare the syllabus for an 18-week course at the new staff school. He laid it down that it would be called a college only if as a staff school it was considered to be a success. With the aid of British and Canadian advisers, the Ghanaians began a junior staff college on Camberley lines in 1964. But this again meant a great deal of dependence on material prepared outside Africa. Most of the senior Ghanaian officers had in fact experienced the real Camberley.

The military training situation reflected a truth common to many African professions. Total integration into the community is not possible unless one is going to abandon all hope of belonging to an international reputation system. As has been explained above, the Sudanese army provides perhaps the best example of a self-made cadre, and it is also the most deeply involved in local disputes. Its officers can afford to run an almost independent training system, because they already belong to a recognizable military tradition based upon the original contacts with Egypt and with the continuation of these contacts through pan-Arab policy making. In tropical Africa, it is difficult for officers trained in the colonial tradition to limit their horizons to the pan-African field.

How far does the common experience of training hold an

officer corps together? Soldiers are obviously better placed to think in international terms than the police. For example, although there has been a considerable increase in the number of non-gazetted police officers trained in Britain since the independence of various African states, the British Police College has not made the same impact on police officers as military institutions on the army.[25] Is educational background and training experience more important than ethnic loyalties in a crisis? Wherever divisions based upon tribe can be contained, it looks as if the experience of training produces yet another set of divisions based on the experience of different generations. Those trained within the framework of the colonial powers' responsibility will obviously view their responsibilities in a rather different light from those trained locally.

MILITARY VALUES AND VIRTUES

The army's relationships with the community therefore seem to encourage a tendency already noted by which the command structure of an army holds itself rather independent of the rest of the public service. In the eyes of the community, the army looks like a lobby which can secure for itself a large proportion of the state's resources. It also contains men who live at the level formerly reserved for the privileged colonial few. This sense of privilege, as has been explained above, extends throughout all ranks, and is not simply a characteristic of the officer cadre. The latter, however, do have the valuable experience of retaining international contacts. While the police force might share the first two characteristics, it can never share the third. Professor Janowitz has argued that the police could never express national goals, and that any intervention in political life made by the police force would be highly unstable and fragmentary.[26]

What values and virtues do the military represent? The army has frequently been described in terms which make it represent an organization far more 'modern' than the state itself. It appears to have its own discipline, its own rules and its own conventions. The military idea of order looks like something

[25] Only 181 African gazetted police officers attended courses at the Police College in twelve years (1955–66), while during the same period 829 black African officer cadets came to England for training. Half the policemen concerned were Nigerian.

[26] Morris Janowitz, *The Military in the Political Development of New Nations* (Chicago and London: The University of Chicago Press, 1964), p. 101.

TABLE TEN

AFRICAN OFFICER CADETS
Training in Britain

Year of Entry	Ghana S	Ghana M	Nigeria S	Nigeria M	Sierra Leone S	Sierra Leone M	Somalia S	Somalia M	Kenya S	Kenya M	Tanzania S	Tanzania M	Uganda S	Uganda M	Malawi S	Malawi M	Zambia S	Zambia M	Centre African Federation Rhodesia S	Centre African Federation Rhodesia M
Before 1953		4	4			1														
1953	1			1	1														1	10
1954	1	5	2	1	1	1													5	9
1955	1	6	7		2														11	5
1956	3	3	2		3			2											4	5
1957	1	1	2		5	3													10	
1958	10	6	5		1		1		3		1								2	
1959	8	2	13	1	2	1	2		5		2								5	
1960	10	3	9	17	1	7	2	15	4				1						5	
1961	8	4	9	34	3	4			2	43	2		2						10	
1962	8	9	8	45		6	2	2	1	21	3	7	1	10					3	
1963	4		9	30		5			9	55	5	8		15			2		6	
1964	4		4			7			7	20	7	18	2	12	2	11	4	11	3	
1965	4								7		6	28	2		2	9	6	19	U.D.I.	
1966	9					14			6	16	8	5	4	8		5	5	20	3	
1967	6					2			7	20	6	2	4	4		4	4	30		
Totals	78	43	74	128	19	51	7	19	51	175	40	68	16	49	4	29	21	80	68	29
	121		202		70		26		226 (includes 12 non-Africans) 1958–61		108		65		33		101		97 (all white except one)	

S = Royal Military Academy, Sandhurst.

M = Eaton Hall and Mons Officer Cadet Schools.

- - - = Break in diplomatic relations with Britain (but Tanzania continued to send cadets after 1965).

close to that of the colonial powers. Military regimes have tended to emphasize the value of economic activity being preserved from disturbances of the peace. The criticisms of the Ghanaian government made in 1967 against its agreement with the American chemical firm of Abbott for the manufacture of drugs in Ghana, brought into the open the conservative features of military thinking. On this kind of issue the younger generation of officers are more likely to have radical views than the older.

The army's relations with the community seem to be governed by the fact that its origin in the process of the transfer of power has given it certain built-in advantages over other parts of the state apparatus. Its organizational needs have been defined by the colonial security system itself, and it has very obvious methods for enforcing its will. But however strongly it may appear to lobby for its own interest, it also provides a point of access to the state apparatus for both inside demands and for outside powers. No army based on a colonial model can hope to reconcile within itself such opposing requirements. Each army tends to contain within it the basic problems of creating civil order, without having the necessary abilities to tackle them. Security forces may represent different mixtures of political aspiration.

The problem therefore of designing a system for civilian control over the army touches exactly the same set of social tensions as the universal preoccupation of government in trying to limit popular aspirations to realistic objectives. As in civilian affairs, the army can either be controlled by some kind of balancing system, setting it against other institutions in the state, or through some doctrine which gives a coherent expression of the purpose of the state. As demonstrated by this chapter, and by the discussion of security policy (see Chapter 3) it is more usual for the new states to control military organization through some type of ethnic or regional balance. Only Guinea, Mali, and Tanzania have begun to experiment with the second method of doctrinal adherence.

From their own point of view, the security forces are caught in a dilemma comparable to that of the civil authorities. As organizations, they are collectively obliged to defend the regime; as individuals, their members may retain loyalties and obligations to sections or groups of society. The obligation to defend the regime looks like an organizational method of self-defence. Like other groups with vested interests in the *status quo*, all with direct access to the resources of the state, the security forces are conscious that they have a lot to lose by change of regime. Soldiers and policemen, like civilians, are likely to be caught up in intrigues or political manœuvres to reallocate the division of resources. Although this situation breeds an atmosphere of uncertainty, in which each individual prepares for all contingencies, they all appear to have a collective interest in retaining the successor state apparatus from which they have been privileged to benefit. The manner in which the public service trades' unions in Dahomey and Upper Volta called upon the army to intervene suggests that they were engaged in a kind of revolt against their own demands, which they knew could not be met. The possession of educational qualifications suitable for holding a prestigious job admits the individual not only to the professional functions of that post, but also to the system of competition which surrounds it. The state is rarely seen as a system of rules, and there has barely been time for established procedures to be generally accepted. The pressures of political necessity can usually by-pass any decisions made by the judiciary. Soldiers and policemen individually are likely to be called upon to represent a system of access to government, just as much as other public servants. The security forces are therefore not only organizations whose instinct for self-preservation obliges them to maintain existing regimes, but also bodies which may express the aspirations of internal groupings or the hopes of outside interests. In the conditions created by the peaceful transfer of power when 'civil order' is in doubt, the organizations of the state share common difficulties. The army is no exception to the rule, although it has a higher chance of surviving the strain.

Chapter Five

NEW FUNCTIONS AND ROLES

THOSE responsible for a new regime after the transfer of
power appeared to undertake similar roles to those played
by the colonial administrators whom they succeeded. But the
forces which had placed them in charge obliged them to perform
very different functions. The new state apparatus was exposed
to the consequences of policy in a more direct manner than its
predecessor because it claimed to be representative. An expansion of the modern sector of the economy under government
auspices seemed to provide the basis of political salvation, and
an escape from the round of competition for public office
between different groups inside the country. But is it possible to
develop a new sense of personal achievement which is not
connected with the patterns of career and ambition laid down
by the colonial education system? Can the regime provide new
opportunities to absorb any sense of frustration or disappoint-
ment? Security policy cannot easily be divorced from labour
policy, when its main problems concern the maintenance of
public order inside the country, not the protection of its borders.
Are there any common elements in military training and industrial apprenticeship, or agricultural improvement? Can military
models be adapted to guarantee the growth of political order?

If the colonial regime was not overthrown in direct combat,
as it was for example in Algeria, the People's Liberation Army
(PLA) cannot provide a model for linking security and labour
policies in a manner which would win Chinese approval. It is
primarily an example to inspire the opponents of existing
regimes. In tropical Africa, where the transfer of power was
usually preceded by systems of election, which provided the
personnel for positions of responsibility, the most militant
organization known to politicians is the party, particularly its
youth wing. The normally open membership of African parties
precluded them from developing Leninist characteristics, except
in a few cases. The under-employed, whether they were urban
or rural, constituted a section of the population whose discontent could be exploited within the framework of electioneering
supervised by the colonial authorities. Politicians found it
difficult to persuade them that their period of influence should

end with independence. A new regime is obliged to consider the question of disciplining its own supporters. The creation of civil order seems to be directly related to the employment situation, but if a leadership enjoys the first fruits of office it finds it hard to preach an example of work. The training course undertaken at one of the National Service camps in Tanzania by the Vice-President, two Ministers, and the Speaker of the House had considerable propaganda value in 1968. How far can the population be mobilized to improve the wealth of the country?

Wherever the state itself has to sponsor an organization which did not exist under colonialism, it has always been tempted to relate the organization's activity either directly to the needs of the regime, or indirectly to the exigencies of international diplomacy, dominated by aid from richer countries. A regime's interpretation of its needs does not necessarily correspond to the preferences of other sections of society. The men or the material which a richer country is prepared to give, or to loan on favourable terms, are not always the most appropriate for the tasks to be performed. The field of military assistance, for example, is notorious for the habit of passing obsolescent weapons on to third-rate powers. The danger to civil order lies in the fact that weapons which are obsolescent in terms of the great power can nevertheless cause havoc if applied in conditions where there are no effective means of reply.

The formulation of labour policy after independence could not avoid using the practices established under colonialism, but it attempted to give them a new meaning. A good indication of this transformation may be found in the attitude of the International Labour Organization (ILO). The latter began to investigate schemes for relieving under-employment in Africa as if they represented breaches of the conventions which had been signed by the colonial powers to outlaw forced labour. Its officials feared that the new states had reverted to practices which were dangerously similar to those which their predecessors had been compelled to abandon through the force of international opinion. They were only gradually converted to the point of view of African governments. By the time of the ILO meeting held in 1966, responsibility for the study of such projects had been transferred from one section of the office to another, international labour standards to human resources development.[1]

[1] C. Rossillion, 'Youth Services for Economic and Social Development' in *International Labour Review*, Vol. 95 (4), April 1967.

In their diagnosis of the problems to be tackled and their application of remedies to be applied, the new governments in fact seemed to be following colonial precedents. The language used in laws and decrees which were promulgated had a colonial ring, apparently inspired by the gospel of work which colonial authorities had stressed. For example, Madagascar in 1960 and Gabon in 1962 both published laws which laid down heavy penalties for idleness. In April, 1964 the Central African Republic decreed that all the unemployed were to be pressed into a 'work army', except those who agreed to return to their villages. There were in most countries two major problems which were inter-related. First, the increase in numbers of people living in towns, without any steady income or prospect of employment, constituted a grave threat to public order. Second, the economic resources of each state were largely dependent on agricultural improvement. Any solution which encouraged young people to leave the towns and return to the villages, particularly with new skills to be applied in agriculture, was acceptable on both counts. The need to provide employment could not easily be met in the non-agricultural sector because of the capital for investment which it required. It is not surprising that governments tended to think that the direction of labour was an appropriate instrument, and that the ILO should be anxious about the trend of events.

The expansion of towns is almost universally important in very distinctive demographic conditions. All the countries of tropical Africa, except Gabon, which has less than 500,000 people, have an age structure which placed roughly half the population at less than 25 years, and at least a third at under 15. Young people represent not only political but also economic salvation. No country has a high enough proportion of economically active people to maintain an extensive system of secondary education. If the modern sector of the economy is to develop, it depends on primary school leavers. One of the principal reasons why a job in the state apparatus carries such prestige was that it provides a source of income which can be used to purchase education for other members of the family. Paying someone's school fees is an easy method of purchasing his support. In some countries, to secure a secondary school place itself appears to be an act of political influence, because it carries with it the hope of public sector employment.

Important differences between countries are themselves frequently the products of colonial boundary drawing. For example, Malawi does not suffer from the same problem of urban expansion, because it has always acted as the rural area which supplies labour for towns in Rhodesia or South Africa. The manner in which boundaries were drawn between Rhodesia and Nyasaland gives Malawi a system which depopulates the villages, and makes able and active men short, but which deprives it of the benefits of urban expansion. Towns on the west coast of Africa tended to attract migrants from the far north. Men in Upper Volta and Niger, for example, were accustomed to finding employment by moving south. In some cases the rate of urban growth was very high, more than 3 per cent a year. Cotonou in Dahomey is believed to have increased more than eight times since the end of World War II. Calculations made to estimate the growth of Kinshasa since Congolese independence suggest that it has grown almost three fold in five years, from about 390,000 in 1960 to over 1,000,000 in 1965. A report published in 1963 calculated that about 62 per cent of the town's population were less than 25 years of age.

The link between labour policy and security policy lies in the proposition that problems of such magnitude can only be tackled if they are treated as military operations. This is taken literally in the Congo, always a prototype for tropical African action, where the army has been employed in the compulsory removal of people from towns and from certain stretches of the countryside. But even without such drastic measures, military discipline might well be applied to bodies other than the police and the army. The colonial authorities had in some cases themselves deduced that there was a connection between unemployment and the expansion of crimes of violence. They had encouraged voluntary youth organizations, and any movement which urged young people to return to the land. In English-speaking Africa, the security committee system always included representatives of the labour department, as well as of the army, police and administration. How far could discipline be given a new significance after independence? Could it provide a new means of bringing the security forces and the community closer together?

PRIVILEGED STATUS OR PRACTICAL ROLE

New states were therefore faced with two broad alternatives. They could either direct the energies of the security forces towards non-military objectives in a programme of public works; or extend the scope of military training to include new concepts of national service. These were not mutually exclusive. A mixture of the two ingredients determined the environment within which the organizations inherited from the colonial authorities were obliged to work. Once again, the police were obviously in a less flexible position than the army. Police work could be performed by new organizations, particularly on the intelligence side (see Chapter 3). But the police were tied much more closely than the army to the whole structure of colonial law. A redefinition of crime and of the judicial process required was a much more complicated process than redirecting the energies of the army. It was much easier to apply the army to new tasks than to replace the police with new organizations.

The degrees of intensity which are possible in applying discipline outside the original framework of the security forces can be divided into at least four levels. The first, and the least onerous, is a system of part-time training instituted largely through the existing pattern of educational provision. The opportunities for syllabus reform provided by independence suggested not only measures for indoctrination in citizenship, but also the application of skills through the schools which brought direct social benefits, such as elementary first-aid in medicine, or increased knowledge about agricultural production. This method was cheap to apply, because existing teachers could be used as the instructors. The Togolese government in 1962 was surprised by the warmness of the response which the course put on by Israeli advisers attracted from practising school teachers. The Youth Movement, the *Jeunesse Pionniere Agricole,* depended entirely on school-teacher instruction. In the first year, 196 teachers volunteered for a six-month training course, at a time when the government itself expected barely 50 to report. The second level is an extension of such a system of part-time instruction to people outside the schools, either as a form of adult education, or as a form of instruction in literacy. The *Jeunesse Pionnière Camerounaise* runs two camps for trainees who fall outside the school system. Both these first two levels of activity have colonial precedents, but the third constitutes an important break with the past. It provides a method of conscripting labour to work on projects of national importance. The most celebrated form of this application of discipline is attached to the more orthodox call for military service. In the francophone states, it is called *Service Civique*. The fourth, and perhaps an application of discipline on a rather different plane, is the redirection of existing military units or the training of special military units to work on projects of social development. Dahomey, like Guinea, established engineering companies for public works. The fourth type implies that soldiers needed training in other directions than the more usual military skills.

In developing its diplomatic contacts inside Africa, Israel advertised its vast experience of the fourth type, the development of the 'Nahal' as part of the Israeli army. The first two types are also closely related to the youth organizations called 'Gadna' in Israel. Although the new states of Africa lack the frontier spirit necessary to maintain the state of Israel, the experience of the 'Gadna' and the 'Nahal' has relevance to the problems of its government. The Afro-Asian Institute sponsored by the trade unions in Israel began its first courses for foreign students in 1961. The first 'Nahal' course for Africans was held in the Summer of 1964.[2] The practice of calling upon Israeli advisers has become almost a habit for youth and education departments in Africa, ever since President Nkrumah called in Israelis to help him fill the gap caused by the death of the first commander of the Ghanaian Worker's Brigade in October, 1959. The extensive tour of African states in 1960 carried out by the Israeli Foreign Minister, Mrs Meir, resulted in many invitations being given to Africans for visits to Israel. Since that date, many ministers and party delegations have been to Tel Aviv and seen for themselves the Israeli movements at work. Their distinctive feature is that the defence forces are built into the everyday life of the people.

This in fact reflects again the contrast which has already been drawn between states which are created by their armies, and those which are not. The 'Gadna' had an underground existence before the British authorities were driven to abandon the administration of Palestine. The Israeli army itself springs from the anti-British struggle. The application of 'Gadna' and 'Nahal' principles to Africa brought the new regimes directly to grapple with the weaknesses of their own situation. The 'Gadna' in Israel, which prepares young people between the ages of 14 and 18 for their period of compulsory national service, is jointly administered by the ministries of education and defence. The nearest equivalent to this type of departmental co-operation

[2] *Shalom, op. cit.,* pp. 20–24.

under British Colonialism was the creation of combined cadet forces in Nigerian schools. Most African states have no experience of linking the army directly with the educational structure. The 'Nahal', which is a voluntary section of the Israeli Defence Forces, made up of those people who are prepared to work on agricultural tasks, is basically a system of defence for new settlements in dangerous frontier conditions. No settlement scheme in Africa can possibly face the same kind of situation; there is no enemy and no guerrillas waiting to destroy the *kibbutz*. The Jewish faith integrates the conscript soldiers and the members of the *kibbutz* in Israel in a way which could not possibly be effected in African conditions. Israeli advisers and African governments know that their problems are not directly comparable with those of Israel, but the type of structure which the Israelis have devised is a most important inspiration to the new governments. Israel has become the most experienced country to provide advisers for African governments on the introduction of new functions and roles in disciplined organizations. Its Ministry of Defence has its own department of international co-operation, which works directly with the Ministry of Foreign Affairs.

The most fundamental policy decision for any new regime was whether or not to introduce some kind of compulsory national service. The indoctrination of youth applied through the schools alone will not reach the whole population, particularly where school enrolment ratios are low. Adult education work rests partly on the willingness of people to attend classes. Yet to apply a system of compulsion costs money. To bring the whole population under the same system of mobilization calls for more resources than the state can normally provide. Some voluntary labour is of course available, particularly if the operation has a certain ideological slant which involves using party agencies. But few regimes have parties with the necessary doctrinal orientation. They tend to be limited by colonial precedents. Colonial armies relied on voluntary enlistment, because they never experienced any difficulty in finding a large number of candidates to choose from. This willingness to join the service of the state is a handicap to independent governments. Political feelings aroused during the period of the nationalist struggle inflated this phenomenon to an intolerable degree. In 1961, immediately after the French hand-over of military units, Gabon, Ivory Coast and Senegal followed the example of their former mother-country in introducing a system

K

of compulsory military service for all young men. The majority of francophone states followed this example. Ironically, the one state which did not need to follow this principle was Guinea, because its national party, the PDG, exercised a sufficiently strong discipline over its members. Guinea had the advantage of a 'clean break' with France. Although Sekou Touré risked the opposition of thousands of former soldiers whom the French had repatriated at independence, he succeeded in building up a new army which was not associated with colonial rule, infused at all levels with the spirit of the ruling party, it was charged from the start with work projects to aid development.[3] The military hierarchy included sections for production, engineering building, roads and bridges and allocated certain jobs, such as road surfacing, cotton picking and peanut harvesting to specific battalions.

All the states which legislated for compulsory service, did so as a matter of principle, rather than as a matter of immediate political necessity. The chief value of such a system is that it provides the beginnings of an effective system of registration among the civilian population, and gives the state an opportunity to choose the best people in each call-up group of conscripts. The law on compulsory service is usually applied by a system of annual decrees, which announce the quota to be filled, the number to be called, and the functions to be performed.

Whatever the size of the school enrolment ratio, the proportion of children in each age group actually attending school, any country which maintained this type of system could choose from the best school leavers. Senegal, for example, used its system of conscription as the main channel for recruiting regular soldiers. Having insisted on 18 months national service, although only from a small proportion of the population, it could afford to build up a cadre of non-commissioned officers, or even officers themselves, from the best conscripts in each contingent. As far as the law was concerned, those francophone states who had adopted this position could progressively introduce a system of compulsion. Tanzania is the only state in anglophone Africa to institute a comparable system of national service. All the others, even Ghana under Nkrumah, relied on the voluntary enlistment system. This sharp contrast between francophone and anglophone practice reflects how difficult it

[3] Victor D. DuBois, 'The Role of the Army in Guinea', *Africa Report*, Vol. 8 (1), January 1963, pp. 3-5.

is to escape from the administrative procedures of the colonial structure. What are the common problems in this field of activity, regardless of the administrative structure?

Few regimes appear to have been capable of endowing their security and labour policies with a common sense of purpose. Even if the security policy remains unchanged, there are many redirections in the field of employment policy. Discipline which is imposed to fight the consequences of poverty faces a very elusive enemy. Any plan to link the employment situation with the security problem touches upon the psychological difficulties of nation-building. A scheme to inculcate the virtues of improved agricultural production may harness considerable energy diverted from the listless life of under-employment, but it cannot easily destroy deeply ingrained attitudes to work. It is quite common for rural resettlement schemes, or for separate schemes to relieve unemployment, to be reformulated three or four times in the space of five years, as for example in Senegal and Mali. It seems to require an obvious outside enemy to unite the government in a single mind of action.

New regimes therefore seem to be faced with two different sets of problems. The first concerns the scope of any venture in the creation of appropriate instruments for development. Success requires almost the impossible, starting at one and the same time from both the government and the remotest village. Bourgoignie in his survey of mobilization methods has pointed out that the most preferable general approach tries to prevent all participants developing a sense of privilege rather than a sense of purpose. He warns against those methods of training young people which are not accompanied by some general in-doctrination of the population as a whole.[4] Anyone, for example, who has been given rudimentary instruction in improved agricultural methods, under the auspices of a national youth organization, may find himself alienated from his own village when he returns, and also resentful of the more highly educated contemporaries who were given full-time government employ-ment. It is dangerous to start from the bottom and work upwards, however pleasing it may be to regard youth movements as the leaven in the system. A badly conceived policy can exacerbate the situation, not improve it.

The second set of problems concerns the basis of recruitment. Because the state cannot usually afford to maintain a system of universal provision, any scheme may develop certain areas of

[4] G-E. Bourgoignie, *op. cit.*, pp. 129–30.

the country more rapidly than others. In some states uneven development is a necessary means of retaining support for the regime in power. It can easily be demonstrated that the UPC areas of Uganda, or the KANU-voting areas of Kenya receive certain privileges in the form of more intensive development, in such matters as health services and schools. Similarly, the establishment of a youth training centre, or a village resettlement scheme, may be a sign of party favour. If national service is not truly national, recruitment itself can be turned into a method of bestowing political favours. A deliberate plan to mix recruits from different regions, placing them together in the same unit, as if it were the army itself, is liable to meet unexpected problems if such units are then applied to building or agricultural work. It is not possible to ride rough-shod over existing traditions in the community. The most effective impact on the local situation in agriculture, for example, may be made by a group of instructors or trainees which originate from that area. But such a narrow base of recruitment contradicts all attempts to instil a sense of common citizenship. When a great emphasis has been placed on the value of bringing representatives from different ethnic backgrounds into the common discipline of work – what the French call 'brassage' – it looks ridiculous to limit particular projects to staff from the same locality. But in the Central African Republic, the Service Civique found that recruits from outside the areas where their training camps were based were sometimes too frightened to move into the strange country roundabout. Similarly, the Ivory Coast discovered that some of their most effective model farms were those staffed directly from people in the district.

Redirections of policy, hesitations, false steps, and expert reappraisals, provide a kind of 'stop-go' rhythm in the field of agricultural extension work for youth organizations, often because of this type of dilemma. These activities also meet another set of difficulties which arise from the type of assistance and advice given by expatriates. Agronomists and youth organizers have developed the widest range of contacts in developing countries, and the new states have frequently inherited organizations which were set up during the colonial period in both these fields. The anglophone and francophone countries have followed two separate traditions. The former adopted the principles of 'community development', worked out by British colonial service officers. These largely followed the lines of voluntary self-help schemes in the villages, super-vised by full-time paid officials. This encouraged the notion that agricultural improvement was something which pleased the paternal eye of the District Commissioner. Francophone states learnt the principles of *'animation rurale'* largely from a set of private organizations based in Paris, several of which had had considerable experience in North Africa, particularly Morocco. The most celebrated was the I R A M *(Institut de Recherche et d'Application des Méthodes de Développement)*. The first Israeli advisers avoided being associated with the paternalism of the colonial authorities. They made it clear that their role was purely technical, and made no attempt to express opinions on political matters. But most of the countries of tropical Africa found at independence that they had committed themselves to a whole series of schemes stemming from the colonial development period of the late 1950s. It was precisely because the colonial authorities had themselves taken an interest in the employment problem, that it was difficult to initiate a completely fresh approach.

The chief difficulty was political. One of the main motives for setting up further organizations was not solely to promote development, but rather to accommodate various groups of individuals whose unemployment might pose a threat to the regime. It was difficult to provide such people with genuine functions to perform which were not identified with the privileges of public office. Offers of overseas aid, particularly in the form of scholarship schemes, or special training arrange-ments, complicated the picture. The majority of governments made rough and ready distinctions between those projects which were going to be expensive on resources, and those which were relatively cheap. If outside aid was forthcoming, then a particular project was more likely to be accepted, simply because it did not add to the already heavy burden placed upon the country's resources. Each country found itself committed to a mixture of different types of organization, with-out finding the time to sort them out into single and coherent systems.

In making an analysis of *service civique*, Bernard Dumont thought that the most important distinction was that to be made between three kinds of objective. The first and the second were primarily to tackle the dominant social problems, unemploy-ment in the towns, and backwardness in agriculture, and the third to adapt the ordinary principle of military service to new ends.[5] All three objectives could be tackled in a fairy extensive manner, with special staffs and special machinery; only the first two could be done fairly cheaply, particularly if problems were not pressing, or if overseas aid was forthcoming. But it was not possible to save money through the adaption of the system of military service. One could make an existing expensive service perform what seemed to be reasonably valuable social functions. But this in itself was likely to be resisted by the security forces.

It is some measure of the problems raised in this field of activity, that most governments attached responsibility for youth not to the Ministry of Education, but to the President, or the Prime Minister's office. Linking youth with military service, or linking employment policy with security policy required a considerable effort of co-ordination between departments. The success of particular schemes frequently depended upon the degree of connection which they enjoyed with people in high authority. The Malawi Young Pioneers were successful largely because of the President's support, and because the other Minister responsible, Alex Banda, the Minister of Community Development and Planning, gave them considerable priority. It is perhaps significant that only a few months before the collapse of the Zambian Youth Service, the President had transferred the responsibility for it from his own office to the minister of Youth and Cooperatives. Most of the schemes required some kind of co-ordination between at least three or four departments, Agriculture, Labour, Cooperatives, and Education, with perhaps a Department of Youth if such existed. If the regime was a coalition in which individual Ministries were identified with different parties, this in itself might be a great obstacle. Togo appears to have found great difficulty in developing its Youth Movement, largely because there was no real co-ordination between the Ministry of Education and the Ministry of Agriculture. In these conditions, there was little hope of restructuring an administration on Israeli lines, so that the Ministry of Defence was brought into close touch with youth and agricultural schemes. People employed in such organizations naturally developed the normal sense of privilege associated with belonging to a particular sector of the government. Making headway on this front called for exceptional powers of leadership.

[5] Bernard Dumont, 'Les Services Civiques Africains', *Co-opération et Développement*, No. 5, March–April 1965.

PROSPECTS FOR NATIONAL SERVICE

Few states could afford to create a national service which required each citizen to enrol in a disciplined organization, not only because of the heavy costs involved in making it nation-wide; but also because of the risks which such an organization might bring to the delicate balance of the new political system. It was a mistake to arm young people without taking precautions against their being used by opponents of the regime. The progress made towards an effective national service system is a good indication of the establishment of political order. Can young people be brought to accept the obligations of national service without getting notions of privileged status? Can traditional concepts of social duty be extended to include the 'nation'?

The first instinct of any regime which came to power through the ballot box, when faced with the need to link security and labour policies, is to resurrect the role of the political party. Party organs, particularly the militant youth wings, seem the most appropriate forms of military organization for the post-independence scene. Local branches, the women's and workers' 'wings', and the study groups which so many nationalist parties devised, have similar features to the 'private armies' of traditional leaders. The history of many parties is full of *coups* and counter-*coups* inside the party structure. Internal warfare is normal; each group or set of people represents a power base from which rival leaders can compete. *Coups* carried out against the state are easily learnt in the context of party in-fighting. Military intervention may represent the fact that normal habits cannot be constrained to remain beneath the surface of national politics, rather than the arrival of a new and unique phenomenon. Even the 'freedom fighter' armies, such as those organized by F R E L I M O against the Portuguese authorities of Mozambique, have the characteristics of party groupings.[6]

The second instinct of any regime which has secured power on terms devised within the framework of colonial sovereignty is to identify opponents by the symbols of their group loyalties, not by an appraisal of their interests. The transfer of power itself effectively guarantees the defence of state boundaries. What needs protection is the style of the regime; what demands attack are the symbols of opposition, however they express

[6] See below, p. 183 n. 3.

themselves. Until a regime is compelled to handle the real clash of interests between states in economic co-operation, or trading privileges, few leaders have experience of assessing the circumstances which bind people together. The three East African countries only learnt about 'national interests' in the detailed negotiations necessary to consider the proposal for federation. The political judgements of leaders could not be formed in statecraft, but in managing to secure local support from local people.

The experience of betrayal is as frequent as the acceptance of loyalty. So many moves are made to guard against loss of face that it is impossible not to translate completely into highly personal terms, or into terms which emphasize the strength of 'primordial loyalties'. 'Freedom fighters' faced the risk of being repudiated either by their colleagues or by those whom they wished to liberate. The Rhodesian police have always been able to exploit the tensions between ZANU and ZAPU; villagers will report the presence of terrorists to the authorities, if the intruders represent a different group from their own leaders. The 'army' sent over the border by FRELIMO into Mozambique will be betrayed to the Portuguese if it contains elements who have been the traditional enemies of the area 'invaded'.[7]

Behind all the attempts to diagnose the causes of poverty, and to explain the obstacles to development, lies the fundamental problem of establishing a system of authority. Those who succeed the colonial administration in running the state apparatus exercise power rather than authority. Their position is subject to challenge. Power expresses itself in the use of force which appears to gain in importance if there are no accepted procedures for effecting change. States created by the transfer of power are hardly likely to be defined in terms of a legal system. When this feature is combined with the habits of personal intrigue which party groupings encouraged, the use of force, as has been described in the third chapter, acquires a kind of magical quality, the ability to destroy the symbols of identity associated with personal opponents.

Behind the attempts to say what type of military organization is appropriate for the new regimes, and to prescribe what functions such an organization should perform, lie the problems of recognizing rewards for personal service or standards of organizational success. It is rare for an African soldier or policeman to be judged by his contemporaries in entirely professional

---

[7] See below, p. 83.

terms. The one Ghanaian officer to be regarded highly for his military competence, Brigadier Michel, who was killed in an accident in 1962, had the distinction of commanding the first Gold Coast 'boys' company' which made him well-known throughout the army. The circumstances in which the security forces are created at independence tend to discourage a direct and regular association between personal reward and the acceptance of discipline; and to make it hard to assess organizational efficiency. If the army is not clear what its role should be, how can it feel satisfied in achieving a defined objective? One cannot easily insert the values of colonial security forces, based on routine and regular procedures, into the uncertainty of political competition which takes its flavour from the 'private armies' inside the parties.

A redefinition of security policy placed the expatriate officers who had designed the security forces in a difficult position, if they remained in the service of a new state. Politicians found that the orthodox procedures established by the colonial authorities were too inflexible to meet their own more personal interpretations of the appropriate use of force. British officers in Tanganyika and Uganda, for example, found it increasingly difficult to undertake the functions which they were assigned. The 1963 clash between Brigadier Douglas, the Army Commander, and Oscar Kambona, the Minister of Defence, on the possible role which the army might play in development schemes became a symbol of the unacceptability of colonial standards. When the Minister asked for a squad to aid a 'self-help' organization, the Brigadier declined to use his soldiers on tasks which he thought were more suitable performed by the Public Works Department! Kambona saw the army both as an opportunity for extending his own power base, and as a channel for aiding revolutionary movements in Mozambique and Zanzibar. The shipment of arms which he secured from Algeria seems to have arrived too late for use in the Zanzibar Revolution.

Yet, at least initially, each regime depended in some degree on the reliability of mercenary-type forces which would confirm the existing government in power. The three East African Leaders found it extremely humiliating to be obliged to British troops for putting down the mutinies of January 1964. But the alternative to outside aid posed too many risks. The new state must begin with a set of instruments which are reliable, because the existence of its authority is in doubt. Any major moves made towards creating a security force based on the national service principle have to come to terms with ideas of reward for services rendered. The task of broadening the base of recruitment or of extending the roles to be formed was a venture undertaken more readily by those who had a reliable force of protection at hand. Some of the greatest experiments in national service training, such as those in the Ivory Coast, have been accepted by those francophone states which rely on defence agreements with France to guard against internal subversion.

Any state which inherits a situation where several forces have a legitimate existence, each with separate organizational commands, faces the greatest difficulties. Each francophone state continued the division of command between the army and the gendarmerie. But wherever such divisions have led to support being given to opposing political forces, the main task of the state apparatus has been to establish a single system. General Mobutu integrated the provincial gendarmerie of the Congo into each *groupement* of infantry in the army. Micombero, after seizing power in Burundi, immediately called upon the Belgians to help him with a plan to join the gendarmerie to the army, and thus forestall the likelihood of this division being exploited by dissidents. These amalgamations carry their own risks. The old units may retain a certain identity inside the new. Jordan could not afford an army on national service lines, and declined to absorb the West Bank National Guard into the Arab Legion, because it would represent political infiltration by opponents of the King.[8] But the state of Jordan itself was in large measure a military creation. The new states of tropical Africa could only retain their integrity by creating a unifying force.

An effective link between security and labour policies meant that security forces were required to surrender something of their autonomy. If a 'national service' system was to help the establishment of an acceptable political regime, the government had to take away from the army its colonial privilege of choosing whom to recruit, and its own definition of the tasks to be performed. To relate the structure and function of disciplined forces to an assessment of the employment situation was the most obvious expression of civilian attempts to control the development of military roles.

Yet the usual experience of those taking decisions in this field was so closely related to the realities of party warfare, that the

[8] P. J. Vatikiotis, *Politics and the Military in Jordan* (London: Frank Cass; New York: Praeger, 1967), pp. 79–81.

outcome of any assessment of the situation tended to mix political motives and national objectives. Of the four levels of discipline mentioned above, only two were thorough-going methods of creating employment, conscript labour on national projects and the redirection of military units into non-military work. The latter method might cause local resentment if soldiers appeared to be depriving civilians of wage employment. In Nigeria it was argued that the army should not help in public works, because its presence aroused suspicion. The other two levels of discipline, youth work in the schools and instruction provided for those outside the educational system, were in danger of arousing ambitions which could not be fulfilled, unless they were linked to decisions taken in other areas of social policy.

In conditions where wage employment is rare, the experience of full-time instruction, or the acceptance of discipline, however light, even if it means only a uniform and a little drill practice, conveys the illusion of entering the 'modern sector' of the economy. One of the first conditions made by Israeli instructors with 'Gadna'–'Nahal' experience when they began working in Africa, was almost universal support for the curtailment of training periods, whether they were in Israel itself, or whether they were in specially constructed camps. Trainees who spent more than three or four months away from their home environment seemed reluctant to return and apply what they had learnt. Notions of personal reward and success were not those of the *kibbutz*! One of the most interesting aspects of studying youth movements is the continuous process of readjustment which seems to be necessary in order to counteract the resistance of the youth themselves.

The acceptance of discipline does not automatically imply a recognition of authority. The whole concept of a disciplined organization in the eyes of the trainees is likely to be very different from the official objective laid down by the state. The construction and development of 'national service' bodies vary with the degree to which the whole economy can meet the demands laid upon it. They obviously belong to the process by which the idea of the state itself is gradually transformed.

The process appears to have two extremes. On the one hand, if the state apparatus can extend itself to include the mass of the people without overreaching itself with the expenditure of valuable resources, security and employment can be guaranteed by a people's militia system. On the other hand, if there is not a sufficient degree of coherence inside the regime for the latter to expose itself to potential threats, the most which a government can generate is limited expenditure on organizations which provide an invitation to modern sector employment. The basic pattern in each country is some amalgamation of the doctrinal fervour of the party, and the opportunities afforded by the economic system. Only Guinea and Congo (Brazzaville) have found that they can establish a people's militia alongside the professional army. Even the confidence which such organizations engender seems to require a further backing of the more traditional type. In January 1961 the *Parti Démocratique de Guinée* in Guinea decided to form 'committees for the defence of the revolution,' on a work-place basis, but methods of recruitment and training of the new militia were linked directly with those of the *service civique*. The great handicap of every state is that it cannot easily abolish inherited colonial institutions, precisely because they provide employment.

The majority of regimes sought to find the easiest method of building their political supporters into the state system. Almost a prototype for newer governments to copy, the Ghana Workers' Brigade, was not in fact brought into a direct relationship with the army until two years before the *coup*. In the government white paper of April 1957, which stated the reasons for its creation, the Brigade was regarded primarily as a measure to relieve unemployment, and to concentrate attention on improved methods of building. Its members enlisted voluntarily, received pay and uniforms, and were organized on a regional basis, one camp for each region. By 1960 its size was less than half that of the originally planned figure of 25,000. In line with developments in other parts of Africa, and particularly under the influence of Israeli advice, it received a new orientation towards the role of an 'agricultural army' which could aid the implementation of a government commitment to 'state farms'.[9] Apart from the ceremonial branch which was used in party rallies, 'state visit' parades, and official anniversary celebrations, the brigade was divided into two sections, agriculture and works. The second major reorientation towards para-military roles was part of Nkrumah's reconstruction of the state security system in 1962–63 which has already been described. By the time military training was introduced into the brigade in November 1963, its numbers had fallen to less

[9] Peter Hodge, 'Ghana's Workers' Brigade', *British Journal of Sociology*, XV (2), June 1964.

than 7,500. In November 1964 it received a soldier for the first
time as its national organizer, Colonel Musa Kuti. His predecessor, J. E. Ababio, was a former policeman. But the
brigade structure remained strictly separate from the army,
and no serious attempt was made to bring it into closer contact,
although the brigade was brought under military law in order
to establish reserve units of the armed forces inside it. The
military regime established by the coup of February 1966
dismantled the other parts of Nkrumah's security system, but
the Workers' Brigade continued to be administered by the
Ministry of Defence.

A much stronger challenge to the colonial pattern of recruitment was posed by any suggestion that party organizations or
youth movements should be used to pre-select members of the
armed forces. The experience of Nkrumah's Ghana was not
typical of anglophone Africa in this respect, possibly because
its army was already firmly established with a high proportion
of trained African officers before independence. The need to
produce an officer cadre rapidly, and the desire to provide posts
for political protégés combined to encourage individual
ministers in ventures for sending officer cadets abroad. The
Kenyan Army under British command insisted on retraining all
those who returned home expecting a post in the armed forces,
before it was prepared to consider them for commissioning.
The Tanganyika and Uganda armies accepted those sent under
ministerial sponsorship to Israel in 1963. Youth movements
financed from state resources were the closest models to former
party organizations which any regime could supply. If it were
possible to establish them as a link between the educational and
security systems – just as the Gadna preceded the Nahal in the
Israeli army – they would not only acquire greater prestige and
a clear sense of purpose, but also provide a greater sense of
identity between a regime and its supporters. It was dangerous
to conceive of a youth movement primarily as a safety valve to
release the frustrations of the 'half-educated', those incapable
of holding the more responsible posts of the state apparatus and
yet unwilling to return to subsistence farming. Perhaps significantly, in the two movements which met this danger, the
Kenyan and the Zambian, Israeli advisers were excluded from
one and voluntarily withdrew from the other. The National
Youth Service in Kenya, established in 1964, enjoyed the
prestige accorded to veterans of the Mau Mau revolt. J. M.
Kariuki, the organizer, and other leading members of the cadre

had distinguished records as guerrilla fighters. It looked at first sight like a people's army to represent the legitimacy of the new regime. Although certain sections of the Kenya government pressed for the youth service to provide the basis for future recruitments into the army, the latter was able to retain standards of fitness and educational attainment which virtually excluded this possibility. When the army agreed in the Autumn of 1966 to accept 90 recruits from the youth service in the next intake of 270, this quota could not be filled. Although the youth service undertook dangerous work, such as building the road to Ethiopia while being harried by Somali bandits, the army succeeded in resisting pressure to provide it with arms. It lost the attractions of a 'counter army' when the army itself became more representative of the regime's desires. The ethnic structure of the Kenya army, as explained above, did not represent a threat to the regime.

The Zambian Youth Service, after many scandals involving accusations of corruption, collapsed in disarray in the Summer of 1967 because it failed to provide significant functions for the UNIP party supporters, who manned its original cadre. The tensions within the party broke the youth service. After German and Scandinavian advisers had failed to make headway, the Israeli training team survived barely a year, only to be accused of 'going on strike' to express their disapproval of its 'shoddy organization'. The most important aspect of the youth service's training scheme was its concentration on industrial apprenticeship. This made it dependent on the private sector, and particularly on the mining companies, if it wished to find places for its trainees.

Youth movements which were regarded as safety valves for the release of political energy inevitably suffered from comparison with bodies more closely involved in the state apparatus. How could they achieve 'parity of esteem' when they were not clearly related to a general policy for making the fruits of independence more generally accessible? If they were not fully integrated into the security forces, their officers tended inevitably to be regarded as of lower quality, and their standards of performance as of low achievement. Nkrumah sent the leaders of the Workers' Brigade to the Ghana Military Academy and the Police College, but failed to treat them on a par with military men. Kenyatta was anxious to demonstrate that his 'youth service' men might provide suitable officer material for the army, but was compelled to admit, after a special course which had been prepared for those he selected, that they failed to meet the required level of attainment. Only 3 out of 33 were commissioned. The most effective way of overcoming this kind of distinction was to give the youth movement the same organizational status as the army, and to introduce some common training course, such as that used in Madagascar after 1965.

An anglophone example which merits further study is the Tanzanian reform of the army which took pace after the mutiny in 1964. The government in this case placed the problem of retaining the army's loyalty in the much broader context of relationship between the ruling party TANU, and the state apparatus. The party youth league provided the basis for the reconstruction of the army. Although the plan to base all recruitment on a system of nomination through party secretaries was not sustained for very long, it provided the inspiration for a 'National Service'. Such para-military training as was given to the youth league itself created the opportunity to set up an army reserve. In fact, the military authorities quickly discovered the need to be selective. Party secretaries had been only too eager to use the promise of an army job as a means of getting men to pay their party dues. The army began in its new form with a new commander, Sarakikya. Both Nyirenda who had been appointed commander by the British when they put down the mutiny, and Kavanna who had been nominated commander by the mutineers themselves, were compelled to resign. The mutiny appears to have hastened the appointment of a special presidential commission to examine the consequence of legalizing the *de facto* predominance of the ruling party. The commissioner's report and the constitution proclaimed in July 1965 led to the legalization of the one-party state in which the armed forces could be admitted to the party structure. A new political commissar in the army was given the rank of Colonel, and each company commander acted as chairman of the party committee elected by his men.

There were two important features in this reform. First, service in the army was limited to party members; second, there was a period of compulsory service in the national youth movement. The army was therefore a body of regulars which could in theory recruit from those who had been conscripted for two years into the youth movement. The 'National Service' admitted about 1,000 recruits a year to its training base from those nominated by the party branches. After three months general training, the majority were detailed to join the farming section and sent out to work one of its regional centres. The engineering section, based at Magomeni, was limited by the shortages of technical instructors and by the paucity of people with technical skills, to taking about 100 recruits at a time for training in public works and construction. About 2,000 of the 5,000 who had passed through national service by 1967 were absorbed into the security forces as regular soldiers or policemen. The army in fact declined to limit its recruitment to national servicemen, although this had been the original plan. The essential difficulty of all regimes was to absorb party loyalties into the apparatus of the state without destroying its effective operation. William Tordoff in his account of the decision to legalize the one-party state in Tanzania emphasizes that President Nyerere deliberately chose the more difficult alternative, to reproduce political competition in the organs of government as well as those of the party. The alternative which he rejected, that of merging party and state completely, runs the risk of losing any vitality which the party organs ever had.[10]

One of the reasons why so much interest has been shown in the Tanzanian experiment is that it attempts to reduce to a minimum the association of a regime with the personality of its leader. It looks like establishing new roles and procedures of conduct. The Tanzanian National Service differs markedly from the francophone experiments in *services civiques* in two respects. It leaves the army to a regular full-time body of men, instead of relying on conscripts; it makes the army a recognized part of the party. These two features are intended to ensure that the army expresses both professional values and political loyalties.

The meaning of party membership for individual soldiers or policemen is more significant than the formal differences between voluntary enlistment and compulsory service. 'Volunteers' under post-independence conditions are not usually raised by recruiting safaris but by administrative or political nomination. Even the Kenya Youth Service accepted one intake based on MPs nominations. The normal procedure in francophone states is for the administration to lay down a quota, whether their recruits serve on a compulsory or voluntary basis, and for that quota to be filled by different regions on an agreed basis. The prefects and sub-prefects of the administration are then responsible for preparing the list of names. This

[10] William Tordoff, *Government and Politics in Tanzania* (Nairobi: East Africa Publishing House, 1967), p. xv.

method of recruitment applies in states of such widely differing ideologies as Mali and the Ivory Coast. The quality of candidates therefore to some extent depends on the convictions of local representatives and administrative officers. For example, it took time for local chiefs to accept that a place in the girls' *service civique* of the Ivory Coast improved the social standing of their daughters. An element of personal choice can become important inside the organization itself. The Ivory Coast government discovered that better results were obtained if boys were not drafted into the *service civique* side of the army. It attempted for two years 1962–64 to run a system by which a two-year conscript spent a year in military training and a year in agricultural work with the *service civique*. It had been hoped that soldiers returning home after their period of service would make a considerable impact on the agricultural methods of the village. After 1964 the *service civique* was converted into a voluntary option for male recruits, while a female section was inaugurated on a 'voluntary' basis. Both continued to be part of the army; the girls' camp was serviced by army vehicles and maintenance men.

Only party indoctrination can hope to counteract the natural conflict between the assumptions of the recruits and those of the government. The boys trained by Israelis in the *Jeunesse Pionnière Agricole* of Togo made it quite clear to their instructors that they hoped to achieve the status of a salaried job, not to continue as agricultural extension workers. The girls trained as monitors to run the Bouaké Training Camp for the *service civique* of the Ivory Coast were annoyed when they were not accorded the full status of *fonctionnaire* or established civil servant.

Both party and government had to accept the power of attachment to local custom. Before 1966 Mali ran two systems in parallel, one for agricultural training which worked with recruits from a defined region, the *écoles saissonnières*, and the other a system of *service civique* which placed recruits from different parts of the country in the same unit. The latter concentrated on a wider range of skills than the purely agricultural. But when the two were amalgamated into a new service of *animation rurale* in April 1966, the regional basis prevailed over the national. The Ivory Coast girls' *service civique*, after difficulties with the first two intakes of 1965, went over entirely in 1966 to a pattern of six-month courses for girls drawn from areas where the work could be supervised by existing youth camps. Israeli advisers in several West African countries, who had begun with ideas based on Israeli experience, in which state-run disciplined organizations provided a 'melting-pot' for Jewish immigrants from many different backgrounds, conceded the necessity of adapting themselves to local conditions.

Party organs, if they were to influence the thoughts of those concerned in training young people and offer the latter a clear vision of their part in the developing political system, had to survive the immediate post-independence period with some sense of cohesion and vitality. The alternatives without party direction were a widening of the gap between those in wage employment, especially if they belonged to the public sector, and the rest; or an increasing dependence of the whole apparatus of government upon a single personality.

The Malawi Young Pioneers appear to have been more successful than the Ghanaian movement on which it was modelled. Although both were heavily dependent on the patronage of their respective Presidents, Banda and Nkrumah, the Malawi organization succeeded in breaking out from the limitations set by the educational system. It followed an adapted Gadna-type of youth movement, which, like those described above as discipline of the second level, combined a reformed school curriculum with agricultural extension work. The Ghanaian Young Pioneers was a school movement in- hibited by the presence of the Workers' Brigade from expanding its sphere of operations. The pioneers in Malawi began with a selection from the Malawi Congress Youth Wing, and used party stalwarts who were not paid for their services as the main cadre of the 'agricultural advisory service' in the villages. About 3,000 people passed through the nine pioneer training farms in the first three years of the movement's existence (1964–67). They all received general post-primary instruction, and were taught methods of improved husbandry without mechanization. Perhaps one reason for the greater impact on local life which the movement achieved, apart from the very skilful Israeli direction, was the persistence of Nyasa tradition that young men went to Rhodesia or South Africa for paid employment.

Just as the T A N U Youth Wing was recognized as a potential ally of the Tanzanian police in an emergency, the Malawi Young Pioneers were deliberately reorganized as a police reserve after the political crisis of September 1964. They were given 20 hours basic rifle training at the two camps then in existence, and told that the police would distribute them with weapons if they were necessary. An 'agricultural' youth movement thus acquired a para-military aspect, which acted as a kind of psychological deterrent to frighten the President's enemies. Even then it was rumoured that the President contemplated setting up a secret camp with Portuguese advisers to mount a 'counter-army'. The women's branch of the party also provided a potential rally of 'amazons'. Malawi politics ran close to the situation of war between 'private armies'. The Chipembere group of ministers which fled from the country in 1964 fought back with military methods. One of their number was killed in an 'invasion'.

The application of military discipline in new organizations after independence ran the risk of reviving not only party faction fighting, which could frustrate any attempt to direct the use of trained bodies of men in economic development; but also the animosities between traditional enemies. A potent factor in determining the outcome of any application of national service principles was the strength of vested interests in the successor state apparatus. A party which means little more than the organization that originally provided the road to power can hardly expect to create an atmosphere which will overcome the natural suspicions of the underprivileged. The army represented to many eyes the height of privilege under colonial rule. National Service organizations were either to perpetuate this impression, or to open up new educational opportunities to a wide range of people.

Chapter Six

COMPARISONS IN MILITARY ACTION

T HE most significant feature of all writing about security forces in Africa is the difficulty of isolating military action from an overall view of the problems of creating civil order. What begins as the study of military organization usually ends as the study of the informal patterns of conflict. In a subject which covers so many dependent variables, it is almost impossible to determine which variable is the most important. How can one compare the different forms which military action has taken in the past five years?

The actual methods used in imposing a government or in establishing a military regime seem much less significant than the basic weakness of all states created by the peaceful transfer of power. A comparison of what soldiers do in order to influence the course of political development is less important than a comparison of the relationships between the state and society. Although all regimes tend to resort to force to express their authority, the strength of any government to enforce its will is very limited.

It is not easy to decide what is necessary to determine the establishment of civil order. The concept itself is difficult to handle, and the evidence is sparse. Disorder in African states under independent sovereignty is still a comparatively recent phenomenon. The rebellions which took place in colonial times did not threaten the state. The personnel of African security forces are still relatively inexperienced in the roles which they are expected to play in independent states. They have not so far shown consistently different patterns of behaviour from other members of the successor state apparatus. Although there is a great need for more systematic work on the structure and background of African armies, particularly their officer corps, it could be easily misdirected and wrongly conceived. Even if one could make direct comparisons on the basis of school background or sense of professionalism between different officer corps, it would still be necessary to determine the kinds of political environment in which they operate.

Some contrasts are obvious. Armies which have been

expanded rapidly for political purposes, such as that of Uganda, admit to their officer corps a broader spectrum of the population than those which remain at their colonial size. Such officers have little time to absorb a sense of professionalism. Armies which have not expanded in size, such as those of Senegal and Tanzania, can afford to be more selective in their training system. But these major differences are part and parcel of the system of conflict, not of any limited military objectives.

This book has therefore tried to relate a study of security forces to the whole context of the successor apparatus created by the transfer of power. A weakness of this method is that it may place too much stress upon colonial design, rather than upon indigenous beliefs. Aristide Zolberg has suggested a more proper starting point in the nature of African society which he calls 'syncretic' to express its dislocation.[1] He sees African states as territorial containers for two sets of values, 'the new', which represent the aspirations of nationalism, and 'the residual', which cover all the distinctive systems of social obligation to be found in traditional society.

The approach used in this book has nevertheless emphasized two important points. First, in colonial days the security forces were the instrument through which the state expressed its main function, the maintenance of law and order. However misunderstood the colonial authorities might be, and however illegitimate their rule might be regarded, they saw their prime function to be the enforcement of law. Second, the main fact of the transfer of power was an over-emphasis on a completely different aspect of the state, organizational rules about the distribution of public office. The state was by and large interpreted in terms of job creation, and not in terms of legal obligation. This treatment of the subject brings out clearly that the western tradition of writing about the state finds it possible to distinguish between two separate levels of activity, and two systems of distribution in the use of political resources.

To reach some conception of the problems facing African governments in the creation of order, it still seems useful to examine the functions of any state in this manner. The first level is concerned with distribution of political resources, or with the establishment of common values on methods of

[1] A. R. Zolberg, 'The Structure of Political Conflict in the New States of Tropical Africa', *IPSA Paper*, September 1961.

business. The second level deals largely with questions of personal power within the organizations of the state apparatus. The first deals directly with the people at large; the second with those holding posts inside government. These two orders of distribution correspond to the two levels described in the first chapter for defining the rule of law.[2] The primary rules of a legal system are concerned with those sanctions which are generally accepted, just as the first level state activity is concerned with resources popularly acknowledged.

But just as a legal system depends upon secondary rules – those rules about rules which, in Professor Hart's terminology, are a necessary feature of any complete system of law – the effectiveness of the state apparatus depends upon obedience to organizational rules about appointments, promotions, and the creation of new jobs. The same distinction can be made when examining the way any consensus is reached. There are two levels for recognizing consensus within a state. The first level is simply general agreement on policies or on particular leaders. Consensus on these terms is fairly easy to mobilize, at a local or regional level, but it is far more difficult when it is necessary to establish a broad consensus within the whole country. At this second level, agreement has to be secured on the legitimate methods of policy-making, and on acceptable instruments of law enforcement. Although it is a difficult method of analysis to apply, this approach makes clear the weakness of African governments. Each regime becomes deeply involved in questions concerning the distribution of posts and the creation of government jobs, which handicap the achievement of secondary rules in the legal system, or make it almost impossible to achieve consensus about legitimate methods of business.

Colonial authorities in the process of transferring power to independent states appear to have based their policy on the assumption that they could themselves create a political class or a political élite to nourish a state and legal system, so that the transfer of power could be peaceful. This rested on the notion that colonial administrators could train viable successors. For example, in British Africa, discussion about the preparations for independence frequently stressed typically English ideas about responsible public service. Perhaps even more than the British, the French system of education emphasized that Africans trained in European methods of thought would be able to embody the

[2] See above Hart pp. 11-12.

secondary rules of the legal system. With the benefit of hindsight, one can understand why the colonial authorities exaggerated the degree to which they could create a political class with a clear national identification. More than any other factor in their experience, the provisions which they made for secondary education opened the eyes of the educated to the tremendous opportunities which would be made available to them outside the traditional colonial framework. Secondary schoolboys saw the world with new eyes, and university undergraduates were frequently able to travel for their education. The natural identification of the new educated class was with their common experience, their standing in the international world of western education. The cult of 'negritude' stems from the black man's consciousness of his inferior status in the eyes of his former colonial masters.

The reality of the transfer of power was very different from that which each side envisaged. The 'successors' did not constitute a coherent political class, or a national one, however much they might have been involved in the nationalist struggle. The latter forged alliances of groups of individuals, coalitions of different parties, and regional associations which cut across tribal loyalties, but in all these different degrees of identity, the ties which were created were hardly strong enough to withstand the strains placed upon them by the extent of the demand for access to a place in the government. Those who got the jobs constituted the new political class, but rather than represent the values of a national system of consensus, they found that they came to be considered individually as stakes in the system on behalf of small sub-cultures or groups.

Those who succeeded the colonial administrators cannot therefore express the authority of government with the same degree of effectiveness as their predecessors, and the orthodox instruments of law enforcement, the civil service, the police, and as a final deterrent, the army, cannot assume that they are working in an environment which respects authority. Zolberg has described the consequences for political life of the phenomenon which he calls 'the shift from power to force' as a technique of government. He thinks that not only do governments become more over-confident in dealing harshly with any opposition, but also they become over-dependent upon any organization capable of exercising force.[3] Any state which does not possess a dominant indigenous political culture is likely to

[3] Zolberg, *op. cit.*, p. 8.

meet great difficulty in establishing a secure system which commands national respect.

It seems to be only in the local context that authority can be demonstrated, particularly personal authority, and restraint exercised in resort to the use of force. Nicholas Hopkins, in his study of the police force in the town of Kita in Mali, has shown how the police chief mediates in family quarrels without using the instruments of the legal system. He calls the disputants together and attempts to reconcile them by persuasion. Hopkins compares appeals to the police with those appeals to fetishes which appear in traditional theatre. These plays present a situation in which a person who has lost property by theft can appeal to the fetish to enter into his quarrel, and punish the offender. The police chief can also operate as a go-between for factions within the party at the local level. Because he possesses the power to call upon instruments of force, he is able to use his position with restraint in a manner not available to national forces. As Hopkins demonstrates in Mali, the local police force act within a system of social control. The whole community of a town imposes a system of restraint on the use of force. Indeed, the ruling party in Mali, the *Union Soudanaise*, organizes its own Youth Wing into its own police force, the *Brigade de Vigilance*. Young men volunteer to spend one night a week on watch patrolling the streets. This force is a natural expression of local community feeling.[4] Any national police force is therefore constrained to operate within a similar set of conventions. Available information on the behaviour of local police forces, suggests that they will identify themselves with the local community in any crisis. The majority of armies are free from this element of restraint.

Some appreciation of the highly local character of folk belief about politics helps one to understand why there is little popular resistance to a change of government by a military *coup*. The army, when it changes the composition of the people in power is not destroying a widely accepted system for the conduct of public business. Support for the previous regime usually quickly evaporates, because previous expressions of commitment were largely artificial. Although they were officially disbanded soon after the *coup* in Ghana, some young pioneers who had been trained on such slogans as 'Nkrumah never dies' or 'Nkrumah is the new Messiah', were seen to march through the streets of

[4] N. Hopkins, 'Social Control in a Malian Town', *African Studies Association Paper*, November 1967.

Accra carrying banners proclaiming 'Nkrumah is NOT our Messiah'.[5] It seems likely that all attempts to arrive at new combinations in existing patterns of belief will only be achieved through the battles of rival machines attempting to achieve some degree of consensus by force.

Professor Janowitz argues that all militarism in these states is reactive, because it has no positive political aims.[6] To understand this military reaction, it is more important to analyse the nature of society involved than to postulate motives which lead soldiers to intervene in politics. One would expect military regimes to appear to return to the norms of colonial administration. The methods of the Ghanaian National Liberation Council, for example, seemed to reflect a desire to rule the country through an alliance of civil servants and traditional chiefs.

There appear to be two major factors affecting the behaviour of security forces which tend to be neglected unless their role is related to the problem of creating political order. Studies which are confined to military motives and to military organization exaggerate the strength of the boundary between military and civil affairs. The different motives expressed by soldiers and policemen, and the different patterns of behaviour which can be found at different levels of the force-structure, are products of the peculiar nature of post-independence experience. The two most important factors affecting civil order are the degree to which access to the state apparatus is open, and the degree to which conflicts within the state apparatus affect the basic function of enforcing the law. Zolberg, for example, has placed his stress in a less legalistic form by drawing attention to two major factors in the structure of society itself. First, he shows that political leaders have to rely upon family, ethnic, or regional ties in order to build up a following. In other words, loyalties which belong to small social groupings become 'politicized' in an entirely unprecedented manner. Second, discontent with opportunities for employment is almost invariably directed against the government, which is regarded as providing the dominant style of prestige and privilege. The two factors of civil order which this book has emphasized can be applied to the study of security forces. The first factor, the degree to which access to the state apparatus is open, can be measured fairly

[5] Jack Goody, 'Consensus and Dissensus in Ghana', *IPSA Paper*, September 1967.
[6] See Janowitz, *op. cit.*, pp. 15, 85–86, 103.

precisely according to their ethnic composition. If the army or the police is dominated by a particular group, or falls closely within the system of patronage of a single faction, it is possible to identify those sections of the population which are denied access.

The second factor, the degree to which conflict inside government affects the community at large, can also be demonstrated in the contrast between those states which experience widespread popular disturbance, and those where changes in the composition of the group in power seem scarcely to impinge upon the lives of ordinary people. A study of these factors affecting order prompt several obvious questions. How representative can the state be of all the different sub-groups within its own territorial unit? When does a dispute at the second level involving primarily different clientages or the followers of small factions affect the lives of the whole community? These questions touch upon some of the basic requirements for an effective state. Questions of access are in practice questions about the nature of communication and political debate; questions affecting the relationship between the state as an apparatus and the state as a people with a common culture are part of the dilemma of creating a balance between the problems of enforcing law and those of organizing government.

It looks therefore as if it is not sufficient to explain the political behaviour of security forces solely in terms of their structure and the motives of their personnel. Any promotion of further understanding of the situation must tackle the major features of society in which the colonial transfer of power took place. How far is it possible to generalize? Can one say, for example, that the more the access to the state is closed, the less likely will security forces protect the civil power, and the more will they be driven into radical revolutionary action? Is it possible to argue that the more the conflicts inside the state apparatus are directly responsible for chaos in the actual procedures of enforcing the law, the less likely can security forces retain their coherence, and the more will they be inclined to act on behalf of sectional interests? These kinds of questions provide some means for relating types of military behaviour to the major factors in the creation of civil order.

This approach can be related to various attempts which have been made to distinguish between different types of *coup d'état*. Huntington, for example, distinguishes between 'governmental *coups*' and 'reform *coups*'.[7] His third category, revolutionary *coups*, in which wholesale changes in the political system are made, seems a rare category in tropical Africa, where only two countries, Zanzibar and Rwanda, have effected such fundamental change by violent means. But his other two categories make sense in terms of the civil order factors. Governmental *coups* or palace revolutions correspond to those conflicts which can be confined to the state as an apparatus or organization. Reform *coups* are characteristic of states in which discontent is directed not against the system alone, but against the groups which happen to be in power at the moment. Governments change by violence; one group replaces another; but none wishes to effect any real revolutionary change. The majority of African states seem to move between governmental and reform *coup* situations. Zolberg has argued that societies in contemporary Africa are unlikely to contain the pre-requisites for political revolution.

Approaching the behaviour of African security forces within the context of civil order, however legalistically it may be defined, helps to get the feel of two general trends which seem to be a remarkably consistent part of the process of the transfer of power from the colonial authorities. First, governments usually need to impose some limitations on the demands made by those whose educational and technical skills give them the privilege of managing the system. The successors of the colonial administrators can only overthrow their new rulers at the risk of endangering their own system of privilege. Second, all governments have to wrestle with conflicting patterns of communication about the definition of what is political. Unless there is a dominant political culture, as in Somalia, or a dominant style, as in Senegal, the uncertainties which face all participants in the political process oblige them to prepare for all contingencies and therefore to exhaust themselves in a vast unnecessary expenditure of political resources.

A government's obligation to meet the demands of the people who enable the state to function, causes real difficulty if the country's economy is not expanding rapidly. Factors which encourage balance of payments problems, or extensive government expenditure without the means to support it, lead the state into the danger of forcing its own civil servants to strike. The army acts frequently as the best organized public service

[7] S. P. Huntington (editor), *Changing Patterns of Military Politics* (New York: The Free Press of Glencoe, 1962), pp. 32–3.

union. The buoyant economy of the Ivory Coast has enabled President Houphouet-Boigny to win his wager with President Nkrumah of Ghana. He challenged the latter's state socialism by announcing that his own open-door policy for foreign investment would provide a surer political background than Nkrumah's attempts at state enterprise and state farms. Houphouet-Boigny has not been compelled to introduce the kind of austerity measures which characterize governments which are overspending the state's resources. Even Tanzania, one of the poorest states of tropical Africa, whose government deliberately encouraged self-denial among the political élite, has experienced difficulty in getting its citizens to accept this degree of discipline.

Any government's attempt to legislate for what is political and what is not, can hardly succeed if a common political language is absent. Governments may set their own policemen against their own supporters, but they remain extremely vulnerable to attack. In 1963, the federal government of Nigeria established an X-squad in the federal police to examine the dealings of politicians, in a vain attempt to limit the extent of bribery and corruption. But the police could be equally venal. President Kaunda of Zambia in the spring of 1967 also announced that his police were to keep an eye on politicians. But no government can effectively enforce common standards of political behaviour through its police system. The irony of the situation is that although force can change governments, it cannot ensure instant acceptance of authority. Governments are weak, not so much because their security forces are weak, but because they lack the power to convince others that their own definition of what is political can be generally accepted.

POSSIBLE SOURCES OF CONFLICT

The range of conflicts in which security forces may be involved has no direct relationship with their size, their superiority in equipment or their strategic planning. When African officers in staff college training are asked to prepare papers on the threats which they envisage, few of them can interpret this request in terms of direct external aggression. The whole environment in which they work induces a perspective which seems far removed from some of the major tensions of world politics.

A few dissidents can change the personnel of any independent regime. Maurice Kouandete, the former *chef de cabinet* of

General Soglo's military government in Dahomey, overthrew his master with the help of about sixty parachutists in December 1967. Professional agitators in the trade union movement in Dahomey had learnt the necessary conventions for inducing soldiers to act. The country experienced four *coups* in a little over four years. The assassination of President Olympio of Togo in January 1963 was effected by a group of demobilized soldiers led by Emmanuel Bodjolle, not even by the seven-hundred-man Togolese Army itself. The latter remained completely passive. It neither overthrew nor defended the regime of President Olympio, either at the time of the *coup* or afterwards.[8] Those responsible for the change of regime were about twenty former soldiers in the French Army who had not been accepted for employment in the new state. Can one describe this action as a military *coup d'état* if the official security forces – army, gendarmerie, and *garde-cercle* – behave as if they are totally uncommitted? Any group which can arm itself – either inside or outside the security system – is able to mount a *coup*. Those inside the system have the easiest opportunity.

Sometimes the term 'military regime' may be misleading. It is possible to argue that the government of Togo, between the assassination of Olympio and the officially declared military *coup* in January 1967 four years later, was an expression of the Northern political strength which had been demonstrated in the downfall of Olympio. Bodjolle, the leader of the ex-soldiers who had struck down the president, Eyadema, the man alleged to have fired the assassin's bullet, who became president after the official *coup*, Grunitsky, the president from 1963 to 1967, and Meatchi, the leader of the main opposition party to Olympio, the UDPT, were all Cabrai from the North where the party drew most of its support.[9] Olympio's strength came mainly from the Ewe in the South who also provided a high proportion of trained manpower necessary for running the government. He had claimed that his own party, the PUT, had the right to represent the 'nation' without in fact extending its base to encompass other groups.[10] The groups which overthrew him established themselves inside the official army. The

[8] Michel Corpierre, 'Les Trois Singularités du Togo', *Preuves*, No. 178, Decembre 1965, p. 52.

[9] R. W. Howe, 'Togo: Four Years of Military Rule', *Africa Report*, May 1967, pp. 6–12.

[10] Michel Corpierre, *Ibid.*, p. 51.

pattern of government was not altered fundamentally by the military intervention of January 1967. Two months previously, some followers of Olympio, including Noe Kutuklui, his successor as leader of the PUT, tried to stage a *coup* against the Grunitsky government. The Army Chief of Staff, Eyadema, displaced the latter in January, 1967 in order to emphasize what had been implicit in all governmental relations since Olympio's death – that the army could exercise its power to break through the tangles of competition for office. He thereby dismissed the claims of rival factions, which had been formed behind Grunitsky and Meatchi, the vice-president.[11]

The dominant characteristic of Togolese development between 1963 and 1967 were the manœuvres of the leaders of the principal political parties in the National Assembly to secure some share in the 'spoils' of office without being able to resolve their disputes through the electoral system. Eyadema dissolved the National Assembly and suspended the constitution. Those in office were the nominees of the military junta instead of UDPT leaders. But the civil service and the main organs of government continued to be run by the educated élite of which the Ewe constituted the most important section. The official military regime was not therefore so very different from its predecessor. Both took for granted the political passivity of 'the masses'.

If a few armed men can take such effective action, they do not need expensive weaponry. When an African army intervenes, there are no tanks rumbling through the streets of the capital, or even armoured cars. The first Nigerian *coup* was undertaken by small 'assassination squads' in the three main centres of political power, Lagos, Ibadan, and Kaduna. No complicated strategic planning is necessary, provided that the government buildings, radio stations, airports and main crossroads can be captured fairly quickly. A handful of men can wreak tremendous damage. Perhaps the only important prerequisite for an effectively planned operation is the availability of lorries for transport, particularly if any military units which might frustrate the action are under the normal handicaps of vehicle maintenance, and are stationed away from the capital. Even the Ghana *coup* of February 1966, one of the most exacting military operations of this kind, was not executed with notable efficiency. In spite of the fact that Flagstaff House, Nkrumah's seat of government, had no proper emplacement for its

[11] *L'Année Politique Africaine* (1966), pp. iii, 31–32.

defenders to use against attack, it took the brigade which mounted the *coup* about twelve hours to get them to surrender. The attackers appear to have had no instructions to use a smoke-screen. A swift and sudden operation can inflict the most damage. The attack launched on the military government by Lieutenant Arthur, the commander of the Reconnaissance Squadron at Ho, on 17 April, 1967, threw Accra into confusion. He was supported by about 120 men who arrived in the capital in four lorries and four Ferret scout-cars. The operation which was dubbed 'Operation Guitar Boy' was directed by the officer who declared that he wished to be the first lieutenant to mount a *coup*! It was obviously more sophisticated in weaponry and tactics than the arrangements made by Bodjolle to overthrow Olympio. Ho, from which Lieutenant Arthur's squadron set out, is close to the Togolese border.

The amount of force required to overthrow a government depends on the circumstances of the moment. Olympio had no defence system; the Ghana military regime could rely on the loyalty of the majority of army units not to join with Lieutenant Arthur. But such circumstances are rarely ones which are affected by the professional expertise of those responsible for state security. Various visitors to Congo (Brazzaville) have described the Cubans who train its militia as a kind of 'prae-torian guard'. Such an instrument affords greater protection from sudden onslaught than a 'national army'. Mercenaries with a commitment to 'the revolution', such as that which has been effected in Zanzibar, and Congo (Brazzaville), are a greater source of strength than local units whose officers develop political ambitions.

It is therefore necessary to extend the study of security forces beyond the different types of sponsorship mentioned in the first chapter. Various exercises in correlation are possible. One can show quite easily the tendency for governments to be changed by military violence in certain types of political system.[12] But few of these attempts at explanation are able to bring together the common elements in a wide variety of situations.

Few of the states created by the transfer of power coincided with territorial units which possessed a common culture. Somalia was exceptional in the pattern of development. The greatest contributory factor to the persistence of a political

[12] For example, see Martin C. Needler, 'Political Development and Military Intervention in Latin America', *American Political Science Review*, September, 1966, pp. 616–622.

style which has roots in the pre-colonial past is the presence of a traditional system at the centre of a new state. While it may be possible to adapt the methods of Wolof people for modern Senegal, it required the destruction of Buganda to enable President Obote to retain power in Uganda. Kenyatta can work out from a Kikuyu base in Kenya, Keita from a Bambara base in Mali. Such advantages are opportunities to transform certain basic loyalties.

Ruanda and Burundi present perhaps the most startling contrast between countries which share a common historical culture – the rule of a Tutsi monarchy over a Hutu peasantry. A revolution in 1961 with Hutu support overthrew the Tutsi system in Ruanda; the abortive *coup* in October 1965 initiated by Hutu elements in the army failed to dislodge the Burundi monarchy. When the latter was finally removed from power by the army *coup* of November 1966, Tutsi officers under Micombero remained in control of the situation. Relations between the Hutu and the Tutsi seem to have conditioned the role of the monarchy in radically different ways. Réné le Marchand has explained the differences in terms of Hutu perceptions of their status within the Tutsi system.[13] He suggests that the greater the perceived discrepancy between objective and subjective status, the greater the obstacles in the way of peaceful adjustment. The King of Burundi appears to have followed sufficiently liberal policies between 1962 and 1965 to avoid direct conflict with the Hutu. But faced with the success of the Hutu *Parti du Peuple* in the 1965 elections, he became exasperatingly obstinate. After the abortive *coup*, the army was purged of Hutu officers. The government became increasingly dependent on the army. The *coup* of November 1966 looked like the completion of the partial take-over begun in July when the new king succeeded. The old King found it impossible to recover from the experience of the abortive *coup* and lived abroad.[14] Apart from the activities of Chinese diplomats, any explanation of the contrast between these two countries must rest on an understanding of the ability of the Tutsi to come to terms with the challenge of running an independent state.

Wherever the new state was granted independence under a

[13] René Lemarchand, 'Political Institutions in Africa: the case of Rwanda and Burundi', *Civilizations*, XVI (3), 1966.
[14] René Lemarchand, 'The Passing of the Mwamiship in Burundi', *Africa Report*, January 1967, pp. 14–24.

federal constitution, it faced the danger of perpetuating traditional rivalries in an institutional form. The peaceful transfer of power rested on the assumption that all the major groups within a territorial unit could be brought to accept a common constitutional formula. But it was axiomatic that security forces could only be organized on a unitary basis. Any break with this principle was likely to destroy the opportunity of creating a new political system. The federation between Mali and Senegal, which collapsed in 1960 soon after it was established, met considerable difficulty in providing a defence system to which both parts would agree. Two-part federations are almost impossible to work. Mali broke off relations with its neighbour over the appointment of the Chief of Staff.[15]

The institutionalization of regional differences tends to extend disputes beyond the level of manœuvres inside the state apparatus. If there are regional governments whose existence is protected by the constitution, all disputes involve considerations which determine the access to government of the people at large. There was a marked difference between political conflict in the Nigerian federal government before the first *coup* in 1966 and that to be witnessed in its neighbours, Dahomey and Togo. All three countries were torn by a basically three-fold division – the north against a divided south. But in the two countries which were not organized on a federal basis, it was possible to construct a government from a coalition of southern interests. After the first army intervention in Dahomey in 1963, Colonel Soglo handed over to a southern coalition with Apithy as president and Ahomadegbe as vice-president. These two men had the support of the two major towns, Cotonou and Porto Novo, and could attempt to ignore the rural north which has sustained President Maga. In Togo, President Olympio built his government from the southern parties and ignored the main opposition from the north represented by the UDPT. The leaders of the Togolese parties after Olympio's downfall in 1963 in fact attempted to reach an agreement on an electoral system to be based on a 'national list', which would have removed close identity between the representative and his region. Francophone Africa has experienced more experiments with the electoral law than anglophone – a reflection of French constitutional experience. Those countries which adopted a 'single list' electoral system, such as Gabon, Chad, Dahomey

[15] William J. Foltz, *From French West Africa to the Mali Federation* (New Haven: Yale University Press, 1965), pp. 176–83.

M

and Togo, avoided the danger of sub-units of power associated with regional groupings, but faced the risk of frequent changes in the personnel at the centre. The Nigerian north had an entrenched position in the constitution, and a built-in electoral advantage, for as long as the electoral law followed British principles of single-member constituencies designed to represent a certain proportion of the population. No coalition of forces at the federal level in Nigeria could be based on the South alone. Indeed, it might be argued that it was only the necessity of giving the North access to the sea and the markets of the South that kept the two parts of the federation together. The North had sufficient weight to enlist a Southern ally.

The existence of military regimes in all three countries might disguise the most obvious feature of this contrast in development. The Nigerian army was transformed just as much as the state by the collapse of confidence which marked the *coups* of 1966; the Dahomean and Togolese armies remained intact. The changes of personnel effected by the army in Dahomey and Togo were largely questions of adjustment in the system of job allocation. But the actions of Nigerian soldiers were symptomatic of much wider feelings of frustration. Military interventions which are followed by a total reconstruction of the army belong to a clearly different pattern of conflict from those which are not.

The discussions which were held at Aburi in Ghana in January 1967 by the Nigerian military leaders had two important features. First, they demonstrated that the military regime found it almost impossible to separate the immediate question of reorganizing a dissident army from the more general issue of the future constitution of the state. The two subjects were inextricably inter-connected. The leaders agreed to implement the suggestion that troops should be sent to the regions of their origin, and divided into 'area commands'. Army agreement to dismantle the army and to deny the necessity for a centralized command came close to denying the existence of the state. The leader of the Eastern Region, Colonel Ojukwu, objected to the post of supreme commander being preserved; he preferred a titular Commander-in-Chief. It is not surprising the leaders placed different interpretations on the discussion after their return home. Second, the discussions demonstrated the fear which officers had experienced in face of mutinous troops. They implied that the only reality to the continued existence of the federation was communication among the leaders themselves, not among the masses. Commodore Wey gave thanks for Colonel Gowon's willingness to take command: ' . . . if we did not have the opportunity of having Jack to accept . . . we would have been all finished . . .'.[16] The second *coup* made it impossible for the senior officer, Brigadier Ogundipe, to assume command.

It is hard in retrospect to disentangle the record of the first *coup* in Nigeria. Subsequent announcements by the Federal Military Government have implicated the late General Ironsi in what amounted to an Ibo plot against the political system. It is alleged that Ironsi knew of the scheme to establish Ibo control, which had been planned in 1965 under the code word 'Exercise Damissa'.[17] But the evidence on this is by no means conclusive, and barely convincing. What is important is that the action of the plotters broke both the army and the state, because they were attacking the first level of state activity, the basic method of allocating resources. They were not confined to a second level reshuffle of personnel. The majority of the plotters were Ibo and a common ethnicity helped to preserve their secret but the enemy they attacked was as much the political system as other ethnic groups.

Events in Nigeria show that traditional enmities can be given a new significance in the post-independence system, and generate feelings of such ferocity that those holding office in the state apparatus cannot exercise control. At the Aburi discussions Colonel Ojukwu was able to show that his command of the troops in the Eastern Region was effective, however illegal it was deemed to be by his colleagues in the Nigerian army. He saw that the only safeguard against the development of 'private regional armies' was an agreement to stop recruitment while the army was divided into area commands.[18]

The military intervention in Sierra Leone after the elections of March 1967 was made entirely on the initiative of the officers – first, by the army commander, and second, by the 'junta' of officers who displaced him. Professor Jones-Quartey has described both events as 'non-*coups*'.[19] A split in the officer corps began to develop soon after January 1965 when the

[16] *The Verbatim Report of the Proceeding of the Supreme Military Council Meeting* held at Aburi on January 4–5, 1967 (Nigeria, 1967), p. 45.

[17] *Nigeria: 1966* (Lagos Federal Government Printer), p. 6.

[18] *The Verbatim Report, op. cit.,* pp. 23–4, 60–1.

[19] *The Legon Observer* (University of Ghana Newspaper), Vols. II (No. 26) and III (No. 2).

British Commander handed over to his African successor, David Lansana. The latter was closely involved with the political tactics of the Prime Minister, Albert Margai, particularly in the policy of developing friendly relations with Guinea. The split began to show certain ethnic characteristics. The tacit opposition to the Margai-Lansana relationship came from officers who were northerners (Temne) or Creoles, led by Colonel Bangura, the most senior officer after Lansana himself. After the arrest of Bangura and other northerners in February 1967 for an alleged plot against Margai, the government and army were closely associated with the dominant tribe of the south, the Mende, to which both Margai and Lansana belonged. Lansana intervened after the election by placing the governor-general and the new Prime Minister, Siaka Stevens, under house arrest. This move seemed to confirm all suspicions that Margai wished to use Lansana's control of the army to remain in power. It looked as if the Margai-Lansana relationship had become an embarrassment to the Mende élite itself.[20] The three officers who led the move to replace the army commander, Blake, Jumu, and Kai-Samba, were all Mende; two of them had married the daughters of Ministers in the Margai Cabinet. A great deal of publicity was given to the last-minute change of plans in the appointment of a chairman for the National Reformation Council which these officers formed. Ambrose Genda, their first choice, who had been deputy commander of the Army until January 1966, when he was dismissed for differences with the commander, was journeying back to Sierra Leone in the company of Andrew Juxon-Smith, their second choice, who had been attending a staff course in England. The decision to take the second instead of the first was communicated to the two candidates at Las Palmas Airport. It has been interpreted as a concession to the non-Mende. Genda is Mende: Juxon-Smith is Creole, but with sufficient intermingling in his ancestry to give him a more 'neutral' status. However, the National Reformation Council looked as if it were Mende-dominated. Jumu is alleged to have attempted a Mende *coup* against the Juxon-Smith regime in August 1967. The overthrow of Juxon-Smith, which was organized by other ranks inside the Army in April 1968, was nailed as an attempt to restore civilian rule when the officers appeared reluctant to surrender power. It is believed that a group of privates pressed

[20] David Dalby, 'The Military Take-Over in Sierra Leone', *The World Today*, August 1967.

two sergeant-majors into taking the lead. They then brought in the two former officers, Bangura and Genda, who had been dismissed during previous disputes.

A remarkable feature of the events in Sierra Leone, when they are compared with those of the previous year in Nigeria, is the fact that all the decisive moves were made in Freetown, the capital, and in Wilberforce Barracks, its garrison. The plotters in Nigeria, precisely because of the federal structure, were obliged to plan a series of simultaneous strikes against provincial headquarters. The brigade headquarters in Tamale which devised the strategy for the Ghana *coup* had to arrange for the transport of provincial troops against the capital. In Sierra Leone the provinces, although deeply concerned, were largely ignored.

Military action in each state has to be understood in the context of a large number of adventitious factors. Because new states are not territorial units with a common culture the forms of political competitions which they develop belong to a mixture of indigenous belief and colonial sanctions which was produced during the colonial period. The accidents of boundary-drawing or of colonial constitution making, established a pattern of territorial relationships which can never be totally ignored.

CATEGORIES OF INTERVENTION

An adequate classification of the types of military intervention in African politics would by its very nature carry an explanation of events. The facts available in this study make it difficult to go beyond middle-level generalizations. Initially at any rate, it seems unwise to classify the actions taken by African armies since 1960 according to the motives which their officers are thought to have shown. Deductions based on an analysis of motive alone would not emphasize the almost structural nature of the vulnerability of the state to subversion. It would need much stronger evidence than that provided by existing studies to confirm that the ideas accepted by African officers have a sufficient degree of homogeneity to justify their being described as a military view of the political system. Even if it were easy to collect material on the social backgrounds of the military, it is doubtful whether the soldiers studied could in all cases be regarded as part of a distinctive social system. Too great an emphasis on the 'life style' of the officer corps is hardly appropriate to conditions in which the same individual plays multiple roles.

Investigations of this subject made in Latin America or the Middle East are usually based on more clearly defined boundaries between the experience of those who join the military and those who represent civilian institutions. The Army in the Middle East has for a long time been a source of political power to which the ambitious would pay attention. Latin American armies have tended to recruit from a distinctive social base in the provinces and to be identified with social forces which are opposed to the radical politics of the cities. Professor J. J. Johnson has argued that the armies of Latin America provided the opportunity for 'small town boys' to break through the limitations on personal advancement imposed by provincial societies.[21] Those educated in the cities were more likely to turn to commerce or the civilian bureaucracy. The colonialist recruiting methods and the patchy nature of economic development in Africa made it unlikely for new states to inherit armies associated with a set of economic interests. The RWAF Force may have taken a considerable proportion of its officer cadets from those areas with fewer opportunities to invest in higher education. For example, in Nigeria Ibo boys from the mid-west saw opportunities in the army. But this phenomenon was off-set by the fact that those areas with good secondary schools naturally predominated in the professional job-market.

The most significant aspect of the African experience of military action in politics seems to be the fact that the transfer of power produced armies which had affinities with the civil servants in the successor state apparatus, with whom they shared common problems of organization and adjustment. The army was as much part of the 'package deal' for the granting of independence as the bureaucracy itself. Soldiers, policemen and civil servants therefore constituted the state as an organization. They received training in colonial conventions and methods of business. Politicians on the other hand represented those aspects of the state which were less tangible, and more vulnerable to dissolution. It is perhaps misleading to imagine that the nationalist movements, which created a situation in which the colonial power was obliged to withdraw, were an effective instrument for building up the state as a people with a common identity. The politicians responsible for mobilizing expressions of discontent against the colonial power depended upon a whole series of alliances which lacked real staying power.

[21] J. J. Johnson, *Military and Society in Latin America* (Stanford, California: Stanford University Press, 1964), pp. 107 ff.

The servants of the 'new state' enjoyed a built-in tactical advantage.

The military regimes set up in Africa have tended to depend heavily on civilian support, almost on colonial lines. The Nigerian army was much too small to govern directly after the first *coup* of 1966 and relied on civil servants to run the machinery of government and on 'leaders of thought' to give advice in a manner similar to that employed by the nominated councils of colonial governors. In local government, the military regime dismissed the elected element in local councils and relied on traditional or appointed members. Ghanaian civil servants were prominent in the committees established by the National Liberation Council, and plans for the return to civilian rule have been devised in a fairly tight circle of civilian advisers. African armies have not developed the features associated with 'modernizing' armies in the Middle East or Latin America which set up a counter-bureaucracy to their civilian counter-parts. Even in francophone Africa where the military claims to efficiency are more obvious, the civil servants have not been displaced by the officer corps. The Ewe élite continued to run the Togolese system under a series of army ministers. Where the army makes some claim to improve upon the inefficiency of the civil service, as in the Central African Republic, the arguments marshalled by army officers against their civil servant colleagues may disguise more deep-seated regional or ethnic tensions. The nearest approach to a military ideology which is intended to replace the 'public service tradition' of the civil servants is the doctrine of military virtue and incor-ruptability. The Central African Republic Military regime in 1966 decreed that nobody who had financial responsibility under the old regime should be re-integrated into the Civil Service.[22] But such bans are likely to be temporary when trained man-power is scarce. Those Senegalese civil servants demoted for their support of Mamadon Dia in 1962 in his bid for power against President Senghor were often quickly promoted into other branches of the civil service.

Within the military command structure, the precise origin of army discontent which leads to intervention indicates the degree to which a clearly identifiable set of values can be ascribed to the soldiers involved. A large number of plots in the army, or other methods of planned subversion, whether they

[22] Alexandre Banza, 'La Remise en Ordre d'un Etat', *Europe–France––Outre–Mer*, No. 144, January 1967, p. 15.

are successful or not, arise within the limited context of *ad hoc* groups or individual battle units, not in the headquarters of the general staff. Many armies seems almost too small to make distinctions between groupings within them; Togo and Dahomey have experienced changes of regime through the intervention of small groups of men. If the army acts as a whole in taking political action, it may in fact appear to be acting as much in self-defence as in support of opposition to the regime. Professor Finer has distinguished between four kinds of motive for military intervention: class, regional, corporate and individual.[23] African conditions appear to encourage the ambitions of individual officers leading specific units, such as that of Lieutenant Arthur in Ghana in 1967, or the aspirations of groups of soldiers from particular regions as in Sierra Leone and Nigeria, rather than the corporate failings of the army as a whole. If there is a strong corporate element in the drive for a military take-over of government, as for example in Ghana in 1966, it suggests that the regime which is attacked had succeeded in threatening the nature of the military institution which the transfer of power had effected. Ironically, it looks as if African armies develop an adequate sense of professionalism only when the state system which they represent appears to be in danger. But this is not the same phenomenon as the 'designed militarism' defined by Morris Janowitz which presupposes that soldiers act together as a coherent body because they share a common objective.

Any survey of recent interventions often seem to produce as many categories as examples. In the absence of any widely accepted system for settling disputes, a few determined men can change the 'balance of power' within the state. The only real revolutions in the post-colonial situation have taken place where radical political energies can be harnessed to the aspirations of an ethnic group which think themselves oppressed by an alien minority. The Wahutu in Rwanda in 1961 rebelled against the Watutsi regime; the Afro-Shirazi party in Zanzibar in 1964 against the Arab minority Zanzibar Naturalist Party (ZNP) government. But the great majority of interventions lack the same finality.

Perhaps the most distinctive feature of the African scene is that the political action taken by soldiers is only occasionally the expression of the army as a whole. The analysis of military

[23] S. E. Finer, *The Man on Horseback* (London: Pall Mall, 1962), pp. 40–58.

intervention has usually been made in terms of corporate action. But African armies frequently display features which are reminiscent of coalitions or congeries of different groups. Any identified sub-unit may decide to take action. This situation is unlikely to produce the phenomenon of the 'swing man', the individual officer who is the last to adhere to the cause of intervention by adding his own weight to provide the minimum necessary for success. Unlike those in Latin America, African armies do not automatically plan a *coup* by the steady process of building up a coalition of 'plotters' inside the officer corps.[24] African conspirators are not faced with such heavy opposition or such high risks of failure. Even where an army appears to be acting as an effective corporate body, as in Uganda in 1966 when the army brought massive support to the Obote regime, it may contain substantial elements of dissent.

It therefore seems important that any attempt to categorize the types of military intervention should make allowances for the rarity of corporate action. Can one establish two broad categories? First, there may be cases of intervention which attract a broad degree of support inside the armed forces. These could well include mutinies by the men against the officers or attacks launched by junior officers against their seniors. When the other ranks of the Sierra Leone army were able to organize the *coup* in April, 1968 which brought a return to civilian rule, almost the whole officer corps and the leading police officers were imprisoned. Second, there may be cases which are primarily the expression of group or sectional interests, but which compel attention by the sheer force of their destructive power. A successful mutiny need not necessarily overthrow the regime if it is not exploited by the regime's opponents, and if the regime's leading personalities survive. The Tanganyikan battalion which took over the streets of the capital, Dar es Salaam, in January 1964, found that the government had 'withdrawn' to safety. But in the majority of cases, the mutineers transform the political situation by killing or removing important figures.

The major arguments of this book have tried to show that the actions of soldiers acquire political significance not from the degree of support which they receive inside the security forces themselves, but from the absence of a political system which can support a high degree of military discipline. The absence of civil order may mean that individual communities inside the state can restrain potential acts of violence among their

[24] Martin C. Needler, *op. cit.*, pp. 616–622.

members at the local level, but rarely that political leadership at the territorial level can renounce the opportunity to reach a solution by violent means.

All governments have to strike a balance between the problems of organizing their own personnel and those of enforcing the law. It was suggested in the first chapter that new states created by the transfer of power neglect the system of law for the system of 'job creation' in the public sector. Earlier in this chapter, the distinction which has been made between two levels of state activity – the level of job allocation and the level of law enforcement – was extended to suggest that there are two major factors in new states which affect the handling of governmental problems. The first factor is the degree of access which the regime provides for all groups in the state to reach the state apparatus. The second factor is the degree to which the conflict for office at the centre of the state apparatus impedes or prohibits the actual business of enforcing the law. Can these factors establish two further categories in the analysis of military intervention?

The first factor, the degree of access, suggests that some soldiers intervene in politics primarily to satisfy either themselves or some other group who feel that they are not receiving a sufficient share in the 'spoils' of the state apparatus. In countries which have an inadequate sense of national identity, it is a cardinal principle that recruitment to the 'bureaucracy' should be based, not on merit, but on regional, ethnic, or party representation. This is government by 'collegiality'. Part of the tragedy of the Nigerian civil war in 1967–69 was that it compelled the most experienced members of the Nigerian officer corps, who had been trained on an all-Nigeria basis, to recognize the 'unrepresentative' character of their composition. Biafra claimed the loyalties of some of the most accomplished officers. Of the thirty-six who had received regular commissions before 1960, sixteen – a high proportion of those from the East or Mid-West – chose to fight with Colonel Ojukwu. Twenty-two of these thirty-six came from the East or Mid-West.

The second factor, the degree to which competition for office prevents effective government, suggests that some soldiers intervene to sustain the processes of administration. Their motives may of course go further than the maintenance of established institutions. The more radical may come to overthrow the political system itself, precisely because its dominant feature was an all-consuming preoccupation with patronage

COMPARISONS IN MILITARY ACTION 177

TABLE ELEVEN

EXPERIENCED NIGERIAN OFFICERS: 1967*
Role in the Civil War

	North	West	Mid-West	East	Total
			Region of Origin		
Biafran HQ	–	–	4	8	12
Federal HQ	2	2	1	2	7
Killed fighting for Biafra or in *coups*	–	1	2	2	5
Killed fighting for Nigeria or in *coups*	5	3	–	2	10
Retired	–	1	–	1	2
Total	7	7	7	15	36

* Those who held a regular commission before independence (short-serve commissions excluded).

(I am grateful to Fitzroy Baptiste and N. J. Miners for helping me with Nigerian sources.)

and job creation. Because they were almost exclusively Ibo, the other characteristics of the 'plotters' who overthrew the Nigerian government in January 1966 have tended to be forgotten. There is no definitive 'list', although some thirty-odd names have been quoted. But eight, average age 27, of the thirteen most prominent had all joined the army after independence, and had a higher degree of secondary education than their contemporaries (two were university graduates; two were Sandhurst cadets). Only one (D. O. Okafor) was an experienced N.C.O. who was granted a commission after independence; the rest were direct entry officers. These characteristics betray an aspect of their *coup* which expressed the mood of the younger generation in Nigeria as a whole.

These distinctions, which are based on the composition of the armed forces and on the major problems of new states, suggest four very general and broad categories into which examples of military intervention might be fitted. None of these categories of course distinguish success from defeat, and like many matrixes of this kind, they produce some strange 'bed-fellows'. But the exercise of deciding the main characteristics of each intervention at least draws attention to the fact that the same country may well experience different types of intervention in succession, and that each example may be a mixture of different elements which it is hard to disentangle.

Any further differentiation within these broad categories depends on a more extensive knowledge of the relationship between the armed forces and the political conditions in which they are called upon to operate. The evidence available suggests at least two general conclusions. First, African armies cannot be assumed automatically ready to obey the orders of the regime in power. The transfer of power gave all military organizations a certain degree of autonomy. There is likely to be a range of degrees of identity with the governments they serve. Second, African armies cannot be assumed to be effective hierarchies of command. The exposure of soldiers to the competing loyalties of other groups guarantees a built-in weakness. There is likely to be a range of degrees of effectiveness in the efficiency with which orders are obeyed.

Chapter Seven

CONCLUSIONS

AN important feature of the new African states created by the transfer of power, which places them immediately in the general category of those subject to violent subversion, is that the state apparatus itself, and wage employment in the public sector which it represents, are the main resources which the new 'political community' possesses. Competition is primarily for jobs, not for changes of policy. It is difficult to avoid a 'winner takes all' situation, particularly if the 'successor class' appears to have been chosen through circumstances dictated by the departing colonial authorities. In the absence of any agreed method for allocating jobs and resources, the security forces cannot remain 'neutral' in the fighting between competing groups. The latter, which are obliged to recognize the state's existence, are not bound to accept the definition of politics and political method which those in power choose to impose.

Even where the regime has succeeded in transforming the structure and ethos of the security forces after independence, to bring them into line with its own aspirations, the fear of military intervention remains. Guinea broke with France in 1958, and was able to build up an army in close alliance with the ruling party apparatus. Nevertheless President Sekou Touré still hesitates to distribute ammunition to more than a few reliable units. Tanzania in 1964 made a clean break with British military assistance, and engaged Canadian advisers to help in rebuilding the army from scratch. But the clash between Oscar Kambona and the President in August 1967 led to rumours that the 'new model army' was not proof against conspiracy. None of the states created by the transfer of power can afford to ignore the constant danger that violence will be directed against the government by those employed to protect it.

The real value of limiting investigation to the immediate difficulties of the transfer of power is that it draws attention to the characteristic limitations on the sovereignty of new states created by this process. The effectiveness of all governments in this situation is qualified by the circumstances of the state's dependence on outside support and recognition. A study of the army and the police touches upon the important aspects of the government's vulnerability to subversion. Inside the recognized territorial limits, the government's power to effect significant changes in the customs of the people it governs is limited by any dispute on the legitimacy of its claim to exercise that power. Outside the territorial limits, its diplomatic strength is determined by a system of alliances which is subject to sudden change, because the regimes of other states are equally vulnerable.

The main conclusions of this study can be summarized under two headings. First, the most pressing form of political competition to survive the initial 'nationalist revolt' is the fight for jobs in the public sector. The most valuable part of the colonial inheritance is the 'senior service', the range of roles formerly occupied by colonial administrators. Soldiers, policemen, and civil servants all belong to the state as an organization, and have an interest in preserving their position which far outweighs any interest in the technical skills they are expected to display. Second, the competition for jobs may often transform old conflicts between the different social groupings which claim access to the new state, and adds a new dimension of rivalry between generations. The atmosphere created by this situation may mean that one secure agreement on the next stage in the transfer of power, the 'succession problem'. Who shall succeed those who replaced the colonial authorities? A change of regime implies a change in the personnel employed by government.

Although these general conclusions can be applied to all states created by the transfer of power, the former colonial structure may continue to influence the exact form of state's vulnerability to subversion. For example, there are two obvious points of contrast between anglophone and francophone states. First, the francophone governments are pressed more frequently to take austerity measures than the anglophone. Second, the francophone institution of gendarmerie poses an additional threat to the security of the regime. The police forces of anglophone states, although important in securing the success of a military take-over, are less likely to be involved in initiating a change of government.

There seem to be two principal styles of budgetary management, which correspond roughly to the division between anglophone and francophone states. The first uses the techniques of deficit financing; the second is compelled by the Franc Zone to employ austerity measures if insuperable difficulties arise. The management of the Ghanaian economy under President

Nkrumah is typical of the first type. In anglophone Africa, the former colonial currency boards which covered East and West Africa, were broken up into a system of national banks. In the Franc Zone the colonial currency system was not destroyed. Except for Guinea and Mali, the whole of francophone Africa came under one currency system, that of the CFA franc, and under two central banks, the BCEAO and the BCCAE.[1] Because the more prosperous members of the Franc Zone, such as the Ivory Coast, are not prepared to endanger the strength and convertibility of the CFA franc, no francophone country can in effect meet a budgetary deficit by employing monetary methods. The rules of the central bank require all countries to agree before any fiduciary issue can be allowed. Deficits which cannot be financed from reserves are therefore only met either by French aid or by special austerity measures. In Dahomey, for example, President Ahomadegbe ordered a 25 per cent cut on all civil service salaries. Austerity measures of this kind are more likely to provoke sudden waves of indignation inside the state apparatus than the mounting inflation experienced by anglophone states. Although the basic problems of anglophone and francophone states are similar, the style of budgetary management can affect the speed of events.

The gendarmerie in francophone countries is in a position to act as a counter to the army itself. For example, when the army in Gabon mutinied in February 1964 and staged a *coup* against the government of President Léon Mba, the gendarmerie, which was still under the command of French officers, remained loyal. Rivalries between different factions which in anglophone countries may split the army itself, can occasionally in francophone conditions become institutionalized in organizational tensions between the two major parts of the armed forces. The police in francophone states is unlikely to play a significant part in politics, although at the local level individual police officers may become powerful figures. The phenomenon of 'rival structures' which has been noted throughout the book is a normal part of the francophone system.

These general conclusions expose the difficulty of meeting requests for advice of a prescriptive character. The proposition that the new states of tropical Africa lack the necessary sense of civil order for military violence to be reserved for external aggression has two corollaries. First, there can be no definition

[1] Full titles are *Banque Centrale des États de l'Afrique de l'Ouest* and *Banque Centrale du Cameroun et de l'Afrique Equatoriale.*

of military policy in terms of civilian control while the regime in power lacks sufficient support in the minds of the people to have an identity which is separate and distinct from the jobs available in the state apparatus. Apart from giving advice in elementary self-protection, which seems unnecessary, one can only recommend a civilian regime to pursue policies which encourage civil order. Yet advice on these lines may look either too vague or too stupid. Civil order is almost by definition the product of conflict, not the pursuit of rational objectives. Second, outside powers can hardly pursue systematic alliances with new states until it is clear what interests such states represent. One can hardly prescribe the principles that outside powers should follow in deciding which governments to support and which to neglect. The fact that outside powers have an element of choice is itself part of the situation created by the absence of civil order. The calculations of outside powers responsible for arms supply or for other forms of military assistance must rely on *ad hoc* assessments of 'friendly' or 'unfriendly' governments.

It is hard to talk of civil-military relations in the African context until it is clear that the boundary between civilian and military marks two fairly distinct spheres inside a common political system. The legal draftsman has difficulty in instituting provisions which make 'civilian control' a recognizable concept. Colonial law tended to treat security forces as if they were 'private armies' in the service of the Governor or his local district representative, and not as instruments of the state. Military law in Africa has rarely been revised, and colonial precedents in military regulations are hardly appropriate. The most rigorous revision has taken place in Ghana and Tanzania where Canadian officers were employed to revise the Defence Acts. For example, the defence force regulations of Tanzania now expressly forbid the Regional Commissioners of the civil administration to treat armed forces in their areas as if they were local levies. Military regimes which displace civilians appear to revert to colonial models, and therefore hinder any progress towards a revision of military law. The military governors of each state in Nigeria behave in a manner not unlike that of their colonial predecessors. The rehabilitation programme in the Mid-West, for example, although allegedly based on American counter-insurgency techniques, has been executed with a distinctly colonial style.

Outside powers in making alliances with 'friendly' governments in the new states face extreme difficulties if there are open civil wars, or unacknowledged foreign incursions. The fact that the new states have hardly any capacity in the manufacture of modern armaments involves outside powers in the question of arms supply for any major operation. Although the Federal Government of Nigeria in 1964 passed the Defence Industries Act and entered into contracts for the local manufacture of weapons, the Nigerian civil war of 1967–68 prompted massive shipments of arms to both the Federal military government and secessionist regime of Biafra. The British government faced an unenviable dilemma in determining the extent of its aid to Nigeria. It was obliged to support the 'legitimate' government and to express a belief in the reality of 'one Nigeria', in spite of extensive sympathy for the Biafran case.

It is impossible for outside powers to avoid some degree of involvement in the process by which states with an effective sense of civil order are created. Their chief interest seems to be in preventing any large-scale conflagration. The major source of friction is still in a sense a continuation of decolonization. Since the unilateral declaration of independence by Rhodesia in 1965, the contest between the power of the Union of South Africa and the rest of 'Black Africa' has been symbolized in opposing forces on each side of the Zambesi river. The southern boundary of Zambia is now the 'front line' in the war for African self-respect. Within this location are extensive opportunities for studying the different bodies which sponsor armed forces, particularly if the study is extended to include the boundaries of the neighbouring Portuguese territories of Angola and Mozambique. There is some evidence to suggest that the three major powers of Southern Africa – Portugal, Rhodesia, and the Union – have already instigated a system of joint military planning.[2] The liberation committee of the OAU, with headquarters in Dar es Salaam, deal with a complex system of sponsorship in supporting the liberation movements. The Congo, Zambia, Malawi, and Tanzania are the latter's hosts. The liberation offensive is frequently bitterly divided between rival groups of sponsors. There are two main armies fighting in each of the three 'enemy territories'. ZAPU and ZANU contest the right to destroy the government of Rhodesia; GRAE and MPLA to outwit the Portuguese in Angola; and FRELIMO and COREMO to take over Mozambique.[3]

[2] *The Times*, March 12, 1968, p. 6.
[3] See *The Times*, March 11, 1968, p. 8. ZANU and ZAPU stand for Zimbabwe African National Union and People's Union; Zimbabwe is the

States created by the transfer of power enjoy certain common features. They tend to be viewed primarily as organizations which create employment opportunities for those with appropriate educational qualifications. Yet they frequently lack the necessary sense of authority to resolve differences between rival groups falling within their territory. The civilian regime which succeeded the colonial authorities may have been able to mobilize sufficient support to provide a basis for government, but it may quickly lose that support when it undertakes responsibility for administration. The characteristic African *coups* are gestures of frustration by the employees of the state or 'caretaker' actions to preserve the state apparatus in existence. There are no equivalents of the traditional alliances in Latin America before 1914 of church, landowners, and soldiers. Some may argue that the large international trading and mining companies constitute a parallel vested interest with which African soldiers might ally themselves. But the comparison is far-fetched. The 'national' armies of Latin America developed from a series of 'private' armies raised by individual leaders. Although it may figure prominently in explanations given for their action, the desire to provide efficient administration does not seem part of the normal African military make-up. There is little evidence to indicate that African armies make better instruments of 'modernization' than their civil servant counterparts. Indeed, all the organizations of the state appear to face a common set of problems.

There is hardly enough evidence at the present time to warrant speculation on the likely outcome of events. It seems clear that the range of political systems to emerge will be much more varied than the initial transfer of power might suggest. If what African armies have done can best be explained in terms of the immediate problems of state organization, what they will do is going to depend on the nature of the conflict arising between those groups which compete for its control. Even civil war is a form of political dialogue when neither side is capable of suppressing the other.

---

name given by nationalists to Rhodesia. The rebel movements in Portuguese territories have Portuguese names which mean 'Angolan Exiled Revolutionary Government' (GRAE), 'Popular Movement for the Liberation of Angola' (MPLA), 'Front for the Liberation of Mozambique' (FRELIMO), and 'Revolutionary Committee of Mozambique' (COREMO). For further up-to-date details, see *Africa Report*, November 1967.

It has still to be proved that military forces can be applied to peaceful uses in such a manner that they make a real contribution to the creation of a stable political system. Armies can be employed in projects which increase the country's wealth or in ways which extend the educational experience of its population, but they can hardly perform such roles without a total reconstruction of the colonial model. The manner in which the transfer of power was effected makes it difficult to avoid providing the armed forces with a sense of privilege and power. The almost in-built autonomy of African armies puts them in an important strategic position in any 'succession' crisis for control of the state. The army faces rival structures which threaten to usurp its privilege or is in danger of collapsing into its constituent groups, which identify with different political forces. The successful *coup* may be either a corporate act or a group action. Neither form of intervention need oblige all sections of society to recognize a common system of politics.

The approach followed in this book involves a certain presupposition about African aspirations. It does not imply that all forms of violence will be banished. It is possible to institute a political system which incorporates various violent rituals of succession, such as the murder of the Sultan's sons and brothers in the Ottoman Empire. But the approach postulates that African leaders wish to reduce the areas of uncertainty. Perhaps African armies will undertake a leading role in effecting the changeover from one set of civilians to another. The state organization can survive a high degree of alienation from the people, particularly if it receives outside support. But the desirability of civil order rests on the extent of political education. The transfer of power at least gives a wider currency to the idea of a new order.

BIBLIOGRAPHICAL NOTE

There are two major bibliographies covering the background to the subject, one by Moshe Lissak in ed. M. Janowitz, *The New Military: Changing Patterns of Organisation* (New York, Russell Sage Foundation, 1964) and the other published by *La Sociologie Contemporaine*, Vol. XIII (1), 1965, as well as several more specialized texts prepared after the *coups* of 1965–66. The latter include 'African Military Coups' (Commonwealth Office Library, March 1966) and 'The Role of the Military in Tropical Africa' (The Brookings Institution, May 1966). The Ministry of Defence Library produces several relevant 'reading lists', particularly on the colonial period. There is a good annotated bibliography by Harvey Glickman in *Africa Forum*, Vol. 2 (1), Summer 1966, pp. 68–75.

David Wood's Adelphi Paper, *The Armed Forces of African States*, (Adelphi Paper No. 15 (London: Institute for Strategic Studies, 1966)) remains the most quoted source for basic statistics and 'hardware'. The CMIDOM (*Centre Militaire d'Information et de Documentation sur l'Outre Mer*) at Versailles publishes an annual cyclostyled list of figures available in France in December, *Les Armées Africaines*. Philippe Schneyder undertook to survey 'L'Afrique Militaire' for the *Académie des Sciences d'Outre-Mer* and his comments and figures are published in the academy's '*comptes rendus mensuels*', tome XXVI. There is an abbreviated version in *Esprit* (September 1967) see pp. 300–18.

Several journals produced special issues after the *coups* of 1966; e.g. *Africa Forum* (Summer 1966); *Current History* (March 1967); *International Journal* (Summer 1966); *Le Mois en Afrique* (Février 1967); *Partisans* (Mai-Juin 1966). There are also several survey articles in *Africa Report* (January 1964, March 1965, and February 1966). Roger Murray's article in the *New Left Review* (July-August 1966) has deservedly attracted considerable comment. In English, the *Africa Research Bulletin* and *Africa Confidential* supply monthly sources of news; in French, there are regular items in *Marchés Tropicaux*, *Europe – France – Outre-Mer*, *France – Eurafrique*, and *Coopération et Développement*. The most comprehensive coverages can be found in *Jeune Afrique*, and in two newspapers from Dakar, *Afrique Nouvelle* and *Le Moniteur Africain*.

By far the most useful journal for military details is *Frères d'Armes* (formerly known as *Tropiques*) which is produced in parallel with the work of CMIDOM, and has no English equivalent, not even among the 'restricted' publications. The details it provides for French-speaking countries can occasionally be compared with those of the English-speaking to be found in regimental journals (e.g. The KAR Journal), the *Royal United Service Institution Journal*, or in training institute magazines e.g. *Wish Stream* (Sandhurst), *Owl Pie* (Camberley). The Ministry of Defence Library has unfortunately not tried to collect together all the new armies' magazines e.g. *Ghana Defence Forces Magazine*, *The Square* (Ghana Military Academy), *Zambia Defence Forces Magazine*. The 'centre de documentation' at CMIDOM has back number files for *Bulletin de Liaison des Forces Armées, République du Cameroun*, and *Bulletin Périodique des Forces Armées Gabonaises*.

There are several relevant collections of conference papers: including 'The Politics of Demilitarisation' (London University, Institute of Commonwealth Studies, April–May 1966); Inter-University Seminar on Armed Forces and Society (International Sociological Association, London, September 1967). Apart from David Wood's paper mentioned above, the Institute for Strategic Studies has also published four other Adelphi papers in this field: W. Gutteridge and Neville Brown, *The African Military Balance* Adelphi Paper 12 (London: ISS, 1964); M. J. V. Bell, *Military Assistance to Independent African States* Adelphi Paper 15 (London: ISS, 1964); D. Humphries, *East African Liberation Movements* Adelphi Paper 16 (London: ISS, 1964); M. J. V. Bell, *Army and Nation in Sub-Saharan Africa* Adelphi Paper 21 (London: ISS, 1965).

The following are the principal books and articles consulted:

Books

Henry Bienen (ed.) *The Military Intervenes* (New York: Russell Sage Foundation 1967); G-E. Bourgoignie, *Jeune Afrique Mobilisable* (Brussels: Editions Universitaires, 1966); Gérard Chaliand, *Lutte armée en Afrique* (Paris, 1967); S. E. Finer, *The Man on Horseback* (London: Pall Mall, 1962); William Gutteridge, *Armed Forces in New States* (London: Oxford U.P. 1962); William Gutteridge, *Military Institutions and*

Power in the New States (London: Pall Mall, 1965); Léo Hamon (ed.) *Le role extra-militaire de l'armée dans le tiers monde* (Paris, 1966); I. L. Horowitz, *Three Worlds of Development: the theory and practice of international stratification* (New York: Oxford U.P. 1966); M. Janowitz, *The Military in the political development of new states* (Chicago: Chicago U.P. 1962); Abdoulaye Ly, *Mercenaires Noirs: note sur une forme de l'exploitation des Africains* (Paris, 1957); Ronald Matthews, *African Powder-Keg: revolt and discontent in six emergent nations* (London: Bodley Head 1966); P. J. Vatikiotis, *Politics and the Military in Jordan: a study of the Arab Legion (1921–57)* (London: Frank Cass; New York: Praeger, 1967); Bernard Vernier, *Armée et Politique au Moyen Orient* (Paris, 1966); Aristide Zolberg, *Creating Political Order: the party states of West Africa* (Chicago: Rand McNally 1966).

Articles

All those in the special numbers of *Le Mois en Afrique* on China (June 1966) and the USSR (March 1967). The reports on Ghana and the Congo in *Africa Report* (November 1966) and on Uganda (December 1966).

Dennis Austin, 'The underlying problem of the army *coup d'état* in Africa', *Optima* (June 1966).

Edward Feit, 'Military Coups and Political Development: Some lessons from Ghana and Nigeria' *World Politics*, January 1968.

B. Fitch and M. Oppenheimer, *Ghana: the end of an illusion*, *Monthly Review*, Vol. 18, July-August, 1966.

William J. Foltz, 'Psychanalyse des armées sud-sahariennes', *Le Mois en Afrique*, fevrier 1967.

William J. Foltz, 'The Military Factors' in Vernon McKay (ed.), *African Diplomacy: studies in the determination of foreign policy* (New York: Praeger, 1966).

J. C. Froelich, 'L'armée au pouvoir en Afrique' in *L'Afrique et l'Asie*, 13–21 (4), 1965.

William Gutteridge, 'The education of the military' in J. S. Coleman (ed.), *Education and Political Development* (Princeton: Princeton U.P., 1965).

Victor LeVine, 'The Course of Political Violence' in W. H. Lewis (ed.). *French-speaking Africa: the search for identity* (New York: Walker, 1965).

Colin Leys, 'Types of Violence', *Transition*, No. 21, pp. 17–20.

A. A. Mazrui and D. Rothchild, 'The Soldier and the State in East Africa', *Western Political Quarterly*, Vol. XX (1), March 1967.

This book was completed before the publication of Geoffrey Bing's *Reap the Whirlwind: an account of Kwame Nkrumah's Ghana, 1950–66* (London: McGibbon and Kee, 1968) and Stanislav Andreski's *The African Predicament* (London: Michael Joseph, 1968). Mr. Bing has revised his judgement that the Ghanaian *coup* of February 1966 was in support of 'martial freedom', the military version of academic freedom (see *Venture* Vol. 18 (5) June 1966, pp. 13–16). He now believes that the plot may have begun with Ewe police officers, and not with the army, and that there may have been outside exploitation of minority nationalist feeling (pp. 435–6). Professor Andreski's book is an extension to Africa of the arguments used in *Parasitism and Subversion: the Case of Latin America* (London: Weidenfeld and Nicolson, 1966). He recognizes that 'corruption' may constitute a system of government which he calls 'kleptocracy', and suggests that recent *coups* can be explained by the lack of consensus in new states on the rights to command and the duties to obey, by the bitterness of the struggle for the 'spoils' of office, and by the weakness of the civilian supra-ethnic organization.

Nor was it possible to benefit from a consideration of the methods to be employed in organizing a *coup*, outlined by Edward Luttwak in *Coup d'Etat: a practical handbook* (London: Allen Lane, the Penguin Press, 1968). Mr Luttwak makes some useful distinctions between formal and informal power, both in government (p. 110) and in the army (p. 62); and describes how to neutralize the army, the police and the security service by sorting out officers according to their ethnic loyalties (p. 71) and career prospects (p. 75). This book is a work of tactics rather than history, and draws on examples largely from the Middle East and Latin America.

INDEX

INDEX